MOMENTUS
Small acts, big change

Hannah Alper

NELSON

NELSON

COPYRIGHT © 2018 Hannah Alper. All rights reserved.

Published by Nelson Education Ltd.

ISBN-13: 978-0-17-684237-6
ISBN-10: 0-17-684237-3

Printed and bound in Canada

2 3 4   20 19 18 17

For more information contact Nelson Education Ltd., 1120 Birchmount Road, Toronto, Ontario M1K 5G4. Or you can visit our website at nelson.com.

"IF YOU WANT TO GO FAST, GO ALONE. IF YOU WANT TO GO FAR, GO TOGETHER."

Hannah Alper, quoting an African proverb

CONTENTS

FOREWORD
BY MARC & CRAIG KIELBURGER

Young people are often treated as "adults in waiting"—told they are too young to understand, too young to challenge themselves, and too young to make a difference in the world.

WE, the organization we founded in 1995 (then known as Free The Children), began as a very small and entirely youth-run initiative. We were 12 and 17 years old, and we wanted to raise awareness around the issue of child labour so we could do something—anything—about it. With a few more friends and classmates on our side, our organization was born around our parents' kitchen table. Since then, just over 20 years later, WE has grown to become a global platform, connecting millions of people around the world who are committed to making a difference and empowering them to go further in their impact.

The hardest part of our journey was when we were first starting out. No one would take us seriously. We were a couple of kids, so what could we possibly know about social change?

But we knew that there were injustices in the world and wanted to do something about them. In those early days, we had called many charities for guidance. One told us that we could help by getting our parents' credit card, and one person went as far as to say that young people should be "seen and not heard." Though this was of course extremely discouraging, we refused to accept what we were being told over and over again—that we were too young and inexperienced to make a difference.

The fact is, one person—no matter what age—can make a *world* of difference. Our organization was funded—and largely still is—by garage sales, car washes, and bake sales run by young people. And in the early days, no one on the board of directors of the organization was older than 18. We've since met thousands and thousands of youth who are full of opinions, ideas, and dreams, and who have committed themselves to making the world a better place, in their own ways. They are idealistic and not afraid to tackle what once seemed impossible and make it a reality. They inspire us every day and are the reason why we believe we have the best jobs in the world.

Hannah Alper is one of those amazing young people. She is living proof that there is no such thing as too young.

Everyone has a gift that they can use to create positive change in our world, be it baking, singing, painting, writing, or running. When we apply these gifts to an issue in order to create change, the impact is extraordinary. Hannah's gift is her words, and in this book, Hannah drives home the message that she has already shared with hundreds of thousands around the world through her blog and speeches—that the only challenge that people (whether they are young or simply young at heart) face is knowing where to start.

There is no denying that taking those first few steps can be difficult, if not outright scary, especially when you are constantly being told that you are simply too young. But making a decision to act has nothing to do with your personal circumstances or level of ability. Rather, as we have learned ourselves, it comes from finding the courage within yourself to do something that might be a little out of your comfort zone.

By doing what she does best, Hannah is changing the world by helping people find that courage. In the process, she is inspiring an entire generation to recognize, and act upon, what they already know in their hearts: that youth can achieve great things—today, not tomorrow, and not just for themselves, but for all those around them. With each word, act, and helping hand, young people are making the world a more just and compassionate place, and as Hannah and so many others like her have shown, there is no limit to how far they will go.

Marc & Craig Kielburger
Co-founders, WE

INTRODUCTION

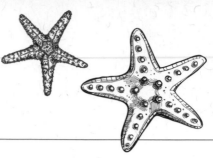

The Starfish Story

An old man was walking along a beach in the early morning. There had been a storm the night before, and he noticed that the beach was covered in starfish as far as he could see in both directions. The old man noticed a young girl walking toward him along the beach. She would occasionally bend over to pick up a starfish and throw it into the ocean.

"What are you doing?" he asked.

"Throwing the starfish back into the ocean," said the girl. "They can't get back into the ocean by themselves, and when the sun gets high in the sky, they will die unless I throw them back into the water."

The old man replied, "There must be tens of thousands of starfish on this beach. I'm afraid you won't be making a difference."

The girl smiled and picked up another starfish and tossed it into the water. "I made a difference for that one."

Story adapted from *The Star Thrower*, by Loren Eiseley.

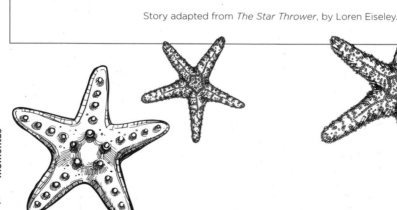
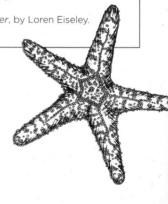

The Starfish Story really sums up how I see the world. Many people, like the old man in the story, think that the many problems we see in our communities and beyond are so big, so overwhelming, that we can't make a dent. But like the young girl in the story, I believe that I can make a difference—one action at a time.

But the girl was all by herself trying to help all of those starfish, and that's not right. I can't do it alone, and neither can you. The good news is we don't have to do it alone. I believe that if there are many of us making small actions, it will lead to big change. The title of this book grew out of that idea. When all of our actions are added up, the impact will be momentous and we will change the world. It is about all of us and all of our moments when we are inspired, passionate, and moved to act—**moment*us***.

When I say "change the world," I'm talking about the whole world, for sure. But I'm also talking about your community and whatever that means to you. It could be your home, your school, your neighbourhood, your city. I'm talking about the people and places that matter most to you.

My Journey

It began on a road trip. My parents and I were driving home from the Digital Family Summit, a conference that brought together families like mine: parents who are engaged in the digital space with kids ready to get online in a safe and meaningful way. Blogging was not something I had thought about before. But I attended a WordPress workshop at the Summit, where 20 of us sat at computers, and I thought, "Okay, I'm here. Why not start a blog?"

It was June 2012, and Carly Rae Jepsen's song "Call Me Maybe" was my favourite song (it was probably yours, too). When we were asked to come up with a name for our blog, the first thing that came to mind was "Call Me Hannah" and the tagline was "Hey, I just met you and this is crazy, here's my blog, read it maybe?" It fit and it stuck.

So, I had a blog and a name, but what did I want to say to the world? Or at any rate, to anyone out there who might read it?

My mom and dad said, "Identify what you are passionate about." I had never even heard anyone utter the word "passionate" until then. I had no idea that this one word would guide me on the journey I am on today.

Identify your passion.

What was I passionate about? I was nine years old, and I loved my dog and all animals. My favourite Disney movies weren't about princesses—they were about animals. I loved going to the zoo and farms and being outside. I was on the Eco Team at school and I looked forward to our lunchtime meetings where we talked about how we could get our classmates and families involved.

I was learning about the environmental issues that animals faced, and I realized that the damage done to our planet affected them, too. All of these statistics about deforestation, habitat loss, extinction, etc., hit me hard. It was so overwhelming. I was shocked, not just because this was happening, but because humans were the cause of it. Animals rely on us to take care of the earth that they, too, call home.

The environment—that's what I was passionate about.

I would blog about the environment and share the eco-friendly living habits I was adopting. Thinking of my school Eco Team, I hoped to inspire others to join me. It didn't take long before I started to see that I was building a community online. People were reading my blog and commenting to let me know they were trying some of my solutions. They were recommending some for me to try, too.

Little things were adding up.

I started to look for organizations in my community and got involved with the WWF (World Wildlife Fund) and Environmental Defence. I loved what they stood for and learned a lot with them. These organizations were amazing to me and always welcomed me. They didn't often have a lot of young people so active. I enjoyed being a part of these organizations, but I didn't realize there was something missing for me until I went to WE Day.

I was invited to attend my first WE Day as a member of the media—to write about it on my blog. I will never forget what it felt like to walk into that stadium filled with thousands of young people just like me. You can't buy a ticket to WE Day—you earn it, through service. Every one of those students had earned their way there by taking action—locally and globally—and making a difference in the world. Just like me.

There is nothing else like WE Day. The energy and spirit that fills every arena is my generation creating change. From the stage, there are conversations about issues ranging from homelessness to inclusivity, from clean water to education. The speakers are always a mix of celebrities, activists, politicians, and youth, all of whom are making a difference. Marc and Craig often say that music has the Grammys, football has the Super Bowl, and social action has WE Day.

Inspired by WE Day, I spent that year launching WE campaigns with both local and global impact at my school and in my community.

Flash forward. I spent two years travelling across North America as a WE Day speaker. On the first tour, I shared the story and inspiration of education activist and Nobel Peace Prize winner Malala Yousafzai, and on the second tour, I co-hosted the Social Empowerment segment of the show. I had the opportunity to meet some incredible people, many of whom I admired, including Martin Luther King III, Kofi Annan, Sheryl Sandberg, Magic Johnson, Chris Hadfield, Selena Gomez, and Demi Lovato. Amazing, all of them. But it was always the young people, my peers, the ones who had earned their way to WE Day by creating massive change in their communities, who inspired me the most. Meeting them in every city was always my favourite.

I had the opportunity to meet even more young people on the WE Create Change Tour in the spring of 2014. It was a cross-Canada tour celebrating the change that students and teachers were making. Fellow WE Ambassador Spencer West and I were joined by Canadian band Neverest, and we travelled from coast to coast on our very own tour bus. Ten weeks. Ninety stops. One epic tour.

What Is This Book About?

If I had a magic wand to create the world I'd like to live in, I'd get rid of poverty, hunger, homelessness, illness, environmental destruction, and bullying—just to name a few. Then I'd add education for all children, peace, kindness, and inclusivity. Sounds awesome, right?

So, I don't have a magic wand, but I do have some ideas, and that's what this book is about.

Throughout my years with WE, I've learned a formula that has guided me. Whether you're taking your first step or your next step, it will help you on your path:

$$Issue + Gift = Change$$

Just like in math, it's easier if we tackle this equation in units. Let's start by talking about the first unit: Issue. That's where I started; I identified the environment as my issue. Your issue might be something that affects people all over the world, or it could be specific to your community. It's okay to have more than one issue—the more people I meet, the more issues I discover.

Your Gift is something you're good at or you like doing. Your gift might be a skill, a hobby, or a resource. It might be something you do for fun in your spare time, or it might be time that you have to give. There are lots of different gifts, and everyone has (at least) one. My gift is communication—through my blog, social media, and public speaking.

So you see how this works. Your Issue + Your Gift = how you Change the world. Boom.

The other thing that has guided my journey is more of a "who" than a "what"—role models. Role models are those people who have set a path and have proved that "it" (whatever your "it" is) can be done. Your role model might be someone you know, such as a teacher or a coach, or someone who has added their voice to an issue you're passionate about, or it might be someone who has paved the path you want to be on.

I have role models in each of these categories, and I'll be introducing them to you throughout the book. As you will see, they have different issues and different gifts, and are each creating change in their own way. I'm so excited for you to meet them.

The last thing I want to mention is that as you read, you're going to see this icon:

Wherever you see it, it's there to highlight an opportunity for you to create change right now. Literally. You'll be able to put down the book and make a difference in that moment. I have placed the icon where I think those opportunities are, but please, if you see other opportunities, take them.

I believe we all have the capacity and responsibility to create change. I don't care how old you are or how young you are, where you live or how much money you have. The ability to create change does not discriminate. It's in everyone.

"We have the choice to use the gift of our life to make the world a better place—or not to bother."

—Dr. Jane Goodall

"BE WHO YOU SAY YOU ARE."

Severn Cullis-Suzuki

SEVERN CULLIS-SUZUKI:
ENVIRONMENTAL ACTIVIST, SPEAKER, TV HOST, AUTHOR

I was nine years old and had been blogging for two months when my mom called me downstairs to watch a video. She didn't say anything; she just played the video. Severn Cullis-Suzuki was sharing a story about how, at four years old, she had filled her wagon with her stuffed animals and walked around her neighbour-hood telling people she wanted to save the animals. Severn was learning about the environmental issues animals faced, and was sad and worried. I totally related.

Then, a video from 1992 showed a 12-year-old Severn speaking at the first United Nations Earth Summit in Rio de Janeiro. As I watched, it hit me: I could do something. I was staring at this video of a young girl not much older than me, talking to world leaders about what mattered to her, and she was making it matter to them.

That was the moment for me. I realized I wasn't alone in this. It was also the moment I realized young people can make a differ-ence, and adults will listen. Young people can change the world. I could change the world.

So Severn was at the top of my list of change-makers to feature in my book, and I'm so honoured to introduce her to you as the first interview. Please meet my first role model, Severn Cullis-Suzuki.

One thing Severn and I have in common is our belief in the power of young people. Severn told me, "We need that energy for the change we have to see in the coming decades. We need that vibrancy, that innate optimism—the hope and the energy that youth has. There's nothing more inspiring than an inspired, articulate, informed young person. It's just one of the most hopeful things there is. The world is hungry for youth to speak truth to power, and that is such an important role that young people can have today."

My issues are the environment & reconciliation.

Severn believes children and youth see and speak the truth in a way nobody else can. I agree. Through my travels, I have met and connected with many young people who are passionate about a variety of issues and speak out about them. It shows adults that we do care about things that are going on locally and globally, that we're not always on a phone taking selfies. We have a voice, we want to use it, and we do use it ... a lot.

> ❝ We need that **vibrancy**, that **innate optimism**—the **hope** and the **energy** that youth has. There's **nothing more inspiring** than an **inspired**, **articulate**, **informed young person**. ❞

We live in an amazing time, with tools and resources to amplify our voices. I asked Severn how being a youth activist 25 years ago was different from being one today.

"We have the ability to find out about others and be in contact with them. The nature of community, an activist community, is entirely different because of the Internet. When I was little, my activism started as me in my own physical world. I began fundraising as a child, which meant doing bake sales and old book sales, trying to raise money for people I knew."

Severn said the only way she found out about other people's efforts was through word of mouth and from her environmental activist parents, David Suzuki and Tara Cullis. Severn explained that the Internet has given young people a platform:

"There are so many youth activists who are very widely known because of their blogs, because of their videos, because they are

Severn Cullis-Suzuki

getting out there in the media through social media. They're able to have a huge impact. This is the era of the empowerment of young people because they can have a real influence in a way that people never have been able to before."

My gift is communication.

My blog has allowed me to connect and share with people from all over the world. I can't imagine not having an online community. And because of social media, Severn's 1992 video went viral, I watched it, and it set me on my path.

One line in her video hits me especially hard. When talking about the harm people have done to the environment, she pleads, "If you don't know how to fix it, please stop breaking it." Those words are so powerful to me. I asked Severn if she thought we'd made progress in helping to protect the earth. She said it was a tough question.

"The world knew about climate change a lifetime ago, and yet here we are. The situation is a lot more dire. How is it that generations never moved on this knowledge and now things are way harder for us to deal with? I think it's a really crucial moment. People are realizing we can't just call for environmental solutions without calling for social justice solutions. I think that that understanding, especially by the younger generations, is very, very hopeful."

It was a relief to hear that word: "hopeful." Knowing Severn has hope helps me stay positive and motivated to continue to make change. In fact, Severn thinks there's never been a better time for radical change.

"It's kind of exciting to be alive at this point in time, because this is a moment where all of our voices actually matter and can be part of gearing our entire species toward the positive story. We need artists, we need musicians, we need people to be the heart of the movement. We need people from all walks of life. We need to give good messages that will inspire a generation to transform. Whatever we're doing, you can play a part."

Severn is saying that we need to use what we are good at to make a difference. I'm pretty sure that sounds familiar. Issue + Gift = Change. Right? And then she takes it further by adding that it takes all of us. Momen*tus*: small acts, big change.

Severn also believes in youth. She told me, "Children are the key to not only actually raising awareness, but heightening people's level of emotional dedication to what is at stake."

If you're afraid people won't listen, keep talking. People listened to Severn. She was only 12 years old when she became known as "the girl who silenced the world for five minutes." Today, inspired by Severn, I use my voice to make change, and so do many others.

The change is educating others.

FINDING YOUR ROLE MODEL

That night in August 2012, I watched the video of Severn addressing the UN again and again. I'll never forget the conversation I had with my mom. I asked her, "Do you think I can do that one day? Do you think I can speak like that and people will listen?" She said, "Hannah, I think you can. Keep learning. Keep writing. When you have something to say, use your voice and people will listen."

Inspired by Severn and everything I saw and felt that night, I wrote a blog post, "Tonight I Found My Role Model," and I realized how important it is to find people who inspire you. I didn't know it at the time, but I think it's fair to say that this is the single most important lesson I have learned.

I have been collecting role models throughout my journey, and I've made it a point to share their stories on my blog. The people who inspire me are one of my favourite topics to write about. Naturally, I have filled this book with role models, and it is my greatest hope they will inspire you. Perhaps some of them will become your role models, too. Maybe some of them already are.

Some of my role models are people who are a huge part of my life, such as Marc and Craig Kielburger, or people I've learned from, like my sensei at karate. Some of them are my friends, like Ashley Rose Murphy, or friends I have made through my travels. The more people I meet—particularly young people who are making a difference—the bigger my list of role models grows.

One of the things I have learned through conversations with other change-makers, some of whom are my role models, is that they all have role models, too.

Severn was my first role model on my journey. She always will be. The night I watched that video, as she told her story I realized we had so many things in common. I learned more about her and the incredible things she had accomplished, and in her I saw the path I wanted to be on. It wasn't necessarily the same path—because we each have our own—but what she showed me was that I could have an impact on the issues that mattered to me, and I really wanted to.

My greatest wish for you is that you find your Severn.

SPENCER WEST:
ACTIVIST, MOTIVATIONAL SPEAKER, AUTHOR

Spencer West has been a huge part of my journey—a role model, a mentor, and a friend. I have had lots of firsts with Spencer: his book, Standing Tall: My Journey, *was the first autobiography (not written for kids) that I read; he was the first person I ever interviewed; and on our tour bus across Canada for the WE Create Change Tour, he gave me advice about my first crush.*

I'll never forget the first time I saw Spencer on the WE Day stage. He said, "I stand here today as living proof that we can redefine what is possible." Spencer was born with a genetic condition that caused the muscles in his legs not to work. Doctors told his parents they'd have to amputate his legs, and that sitting up, walking, or being a functioning member of society would probably be impossible.

As it turned out, there wasn't much Spencer couldn't do. He went to school with his friends and was on the cheer team in high school—he does cartwheels as well as anyone. He went to university and has a great job. Spencer's life has been about redefining possible.

My issue is poverty.

Spencer travels all over the world as a motivational speaker for ME to WE. He told me he has one goal in mind when he speaks to people, whether it's to a small group of business people or a stadium of 20,000 youth.

"The goal has always been to use myself as an example of: 'Listen, we've all got challenges. You can physically see mine, at least some of them. Challenges can be dealt with in different ways, and you can also give back to the world at the same time.' My goal is not to be an inspiration. My goal is to be 'Here's what I can do. Let's see what you can do.'"

I've seen Spencer speak hundreds of times, and this message is always clear from the very beginning from the way he introduces himself:

"I'm an author, motivational speaker, son, and brother. I'm an uncle and somebody who wants to be a dad someday. I'm an activist and someone who doesn't have legs."

Spencer gets around in his wheelchair, and when he was a young boy, he learned to walk on his hands. That might be the first thing you notice when you see Spencer, but it's not who he is. People are so much more than what you see.

> **My goal is not to be an inspiration.**
> **My goal is to be 'Here's what**
> **I can do. Let's see what you can do.'**

By the time I met Spencer, he had been motivating people—especially young people—all over the world to face challenges head on, to uncover their passions and their abilities, and to raise awareness and money for causes they cared about. Through all of that, though, Spencer realized he needed to do the same, and he had a plan. Together with his two best friends, David and Alex, he was going to climb Mount Kilimanjaro in support of access to clean water in Kenya.

Fast-forward to June 2012 when I watched as they made it to the summit. Spencer said it was harder than they had ever imagined, but they did it. I asked him if that was the hardest thing he'd ever done.

"There are two things that I think are harder than that. The first one was figuring out how to find meaning in this life and have a career at the same time, because, be honest, you have to have money to work. How do we earn a living and also give back at the same time?"

My gift is my voice.

Spencer found the answer to that question when a friend asked him to join him on a trip.

Spencer told me it was during a point in his life when he wasn't feeling particularly happy. He had always thought going to school, getting a degree, and making money would bring happiness. That's what most people do, right? But he was not really fulfilled and didn't know what to do. Then his friend Reed invited him to go to Kenya with WE to build a school.

"Seeing this organization helping these community members so they could help themselves was so inspiring, and I suddenly started finding myself asking questions I'd never asked before and becoming interested in things I had no idea I was interested in. It unlocked this whole part of me I didn't know was there."

I know how that feels. It's what happens when you go to Kenya—or really, any time you step outside your life and truly see other people. You don't have to go all the way to Kenya, because there are people and communities doing important work and creating much-needed change closer to home, too. (But if you want to go to Kenya, and you can, Spencer and I highly recommend it!)

Spencer offered great advice for people who want to make a difference.

"What works for me is looking for the things that I love to do. In school, I got good marks, but my report cards would always say, 'Spencer's a great student, but he talks too much.' So I took this idea of telling stories and talking too much and eventually I found something I was passionate about, which is WE and development work and empowerment. I think it's looking for those things, because this work can be daunting and overwhelming if you can't have some fun and enjoy it at the same time."

True story: Spencer once called me "the voice of reason." Okay, it might have been in a script, but he said it. It's on video, so there's proof! I'm going to hand that title off to him now, though, because he truly is the voice of reason. Mic drop.

The change is breaking the cycle of poverty through education.

Spencer West

NO CAN'T. NO WON'T. ONLY HOW.

It's easy to look at people and make assumptions about who they are and what they can or can't do. This goes for anything and everything that you can see on the outside, from what we wear to our weight, skin colour, height, and other physical distinctions. Happens all the time, right? You see someone who's really tall and imagine they'd make a great basketball player, or you look at someone who's really short and think there's no way they could be a great basketball player. I know I'm really simplifying my point here, but sometimes you need to go back to basics and build from there. How we look physically doesn't define us.

Spencer's parents were once told he would never walk. Yet Spencer has climbed Mount Kilimanjaro, the highest mountain in Africa. When we let others set our limitations, we run the risk of becoming them. Set *your own* limitations. Redefine *your* possible.

Spencer lives his life redefining his possible and motivating others to find theirs. To every challenge or obstacle, he says this: "No *can't*. No *won't*. Only *how*." When he focuses on the *how*, he realizes he can do all the things about which he was told "you can't" and "you won't." There are solutions for every challenge or obstacle, and if your mind and heart are open, you'll find them.

Something else we can learn from Spencer is that support is important for both finding solutions and putting them into action. When he was a young boy, Spencer and his family used to spend

time in the summer at an aunt's cottage. All the kids would go swimming, and Spencer could only hang out in the water with inflatable water wings. He told his mom he wanted to swim with his cousins. She found a teacher, and Spencer had private swimming lessons. By the next summer, off came the water wings. Spencer swam with his cousins.

Back to Mount Kilimanjaro. Spencer, David, and Alex spent a year learning what it would take to get to the top, as well as training to prepare for their climb. They were not professional climbers—but they weren't hobby climbers, either. They had a team to guide them on their journey. Spencer understood that he would be making the climb in his wheelchair and walking on his hands, and that there would be times he would need to be carried by his friends or the guide due to the rugged nature of the terrain.

The closer they got to the top of the mountain, the clearer it became to Spencer that David and Alex were suffering from altitude sickness and couldn't walk more than a couple of steps without throwing up. Spencer said it was the one time in his life he wished he had legs so that he could carry his friends. But he knew there was more than one way to carry them. As they neared the summit, in the snow, Spencer said to the guide who was carrying him, "You've got to put me down." Spencer paused with David and Alex, and I don't know exactly what he said in those personal moments with his friends, but what the three of them did next was walk, one step at a time, to that glorious green welcome sign at the top of the highest mountain in Africa.

Spencer's Mount Kilimanjaro campaign raised more than half a million dollars, providing 12,500 people in the WE communities in Kenya with clean water for life.

No *can't*. No *won't*. Only *how*.

"DON'T BE ASHAMED OF WHAT MAKES YOU UNIQUE. ROCK YOUR DIFFERENCES. OWN THEM. AND BE YOU."

Ashley Rose Murphy

ASHLEY ROSE MURPHY:
HIV/AIDS ACTIVIST, MOTIVATIONAL SPEAKER, WE AMBASSADOR

Ashley Rose Murphy is a fighter. She was born HIV positive, and when she was a baby, her condition developed into AIDS. Doctors put her into a coma, and after three months, she was placed with foster parents: Kari and Don Murphy, who are now her adoptive parents. Doctors told Kari and Don that Ashley had only weeks to live. I love what Ashley, who is now 19, says about that: "Clearly, I had other plans." Oh, yes, she did!

Ashley has been a voice and advocate for HIV/AIDS awareness since she was 10 years old. She inspires the world to become more educated about and understanding of those who have HIV/AIDS but are too afraid to speak out and motivates people of all ages to know that they can make a difference.

In her quest to reduce the death toll of AIDS and the stigma associated with having HIV, Ashley has travelled around the world partnering with organizations such as WE, (RED), UNAIDS, Lokai, #GenEndIt, and the Elizabeth Glaser Pediatric AIDS Foundation.

Ashley is one of my greatest inspirations. She is also one of my best friends.

Ashley told me one of the biggest moments of her life was being told she was HIV positive. She was seven years old.

"The doctors thought that seven was an appropriate time for me to know because you can really grasp the information at that age. My parents told me not to tell anybody because they were afraid I would be bullied or stigmatized."

Ashley was 10 when she realized she needed to tell her story. She didn't want to keep it a secret.

"When I heard there were people who were not very knowledgeable about HIV and AIDS, I felt like I should do something. While other kids didn't want to speak out and get their picture taken, I was just like, 'You can put my face anywhere and everywhere.' It makes sense that I want to be an actress! I want to make HIV and AIDS something we don't have to be afraid of anymore."

What Is HIV/AIDS?

HIV stands for "human immunodeficiency virus." HIV is a virus that attacks a person's immune system. When your immune system is broken down, your body can't fight off infections, disease, and other viruses. AIDS (acquired immunodeficiency syndrome) is the most advanced stage of infection caused by HIV.

momentus

Today, Ashley openly shares her story. However, she didn't tell that many people at the beginning of high school, which made speaking at WE Day when she was 16 years old daunting.

"I found it to be very scary that I was telling my story to 16,000 people at one time."

Once she started advocating, Ashley grew more confident and became friends with people who loved her for who she is.

"People would know me as the girl with HIV, and I have no problem telling anybody. I'm just teaching them. I don't shy away from the conversation."

It wasn't always easy. She understood that what she had to do was teach people and dispel the many myths around HIV.

Ashley said because of increased awareness, most people are understanding, but she has received many rude and ignorant comments online and on social media. Ashley expressed that it does get to her sometimes, but she doesn't dwell on it. She knows the real reason for the hate is ignorance—people are not educated and don't understand.

"I feel like because I get these reactions, it keeps me even more motivated to speak out. I feel that if there are people with this kind of mindset and with this ignorance, I still have a job to do, and my job isn't done until the stigma is completely gone, until HIV is completely gone, until there's a cure."

My issue is HIV/AIDS.

My gift is my voice.

Role models are something I truly believe in. They shape who you are and inspire your passions and spark. Ashley's adoptive mom, Kari, is her role model. Kari has fostered 13 children and has been legal guardian to three over the past 12 years. Kari herself was inspired by her own parents, who fostered 184 children over 30 years. Ashley told me her mom has the biggest heart of anyone she's ever met.

"She recognizes that all of us have something that is out of the ordinary. We have stories that prove it, but we are still a normal family with special circumstances. She always taught us, no matter what, to be ourselves."

Today, Ashley is as healthy as can be. She takes one pill per day to treat her condition. She is a theatre student at York University and aspires to be an actress. Pretty awesome when you remember that doctors didn't expect her to live to celebrate her first birthday! In fact, Ashley celebrated her 18th birthday in Los Angeles at an all-night dance party raising funds for the Elizabeth Glaser Pediatric AIDS Foundation, and the next day she was on stage at WE Day with Charlize Theron, who prompted the 18,000-strong crowd to sing "Happy Birthday."

Ashley most recently teamed up with Theron for #GenEndIt, a movement that aims to end HIV and AIDS by 2030. Ashley is hopeful. "That's 13 years away. And where we are right now, I feel like it might be possible."

With her activism, Ashley hopes not just to educate and inspire people but also to make a person's day better.

"If I could make someone's day better, if I could help someone with whatever they're going through, whether that's a mental health issue or if it is HIV and AIDS and they want to come out, but they're too afraid to, I'll try. I want to help those who are voiceless, who are too afraid to speak out, and I want them to realize through my story, and how I've overcome so much, that they can overcome, as well."

One of the many things I love about Ashley is her positive outlook on life. Over the years, she has given many interviews, and when someone asked her if she would rather not have HIV, this is what she said:

"If I wasn't in these circumstances, I would not have met the people I've met. I wouldn't have been with the family I'm with."

This statement is everything that Ashley is—gratitude and family, love and acceptance.

The changes are educating people & spreading awareness about HIV/AIDS.

IT'S NOT ALWAYS SUNSHINE AND RAINBOWS

I love what I do, and I firmly believe in the things I stand for, the things that I stand up for. I believe my voice matters, and I have never been afraid to use it. I've had some incredible experiences and opportunities throughout my journey and have met some really awesome people. I have met musicians, actors, world leaders, and activists of all ages. I have had the best geography and history lessons because I've travelled. There is no better way to really know Canada than travelling across it in a bus from coast to coast meeting students and teachers all over our country. I have given keynote speeches in New York, California, Kentucky, Texas, Las Vegas, and more. I have spent time in Kenya and gained a true understanding of global development. Even recounting this here and now, I know that I have an amazing life.

But I want to tell you something—it's not easy. There is hard work and a hard reality for me. I'm going to be totally honest and very vulnerable and tell you a little bit about my personal life.

One of the hardest things for me has been my social life, especially at school. When I'm speaking or participating in events—big or small—I'm always very aware that I'm surrounded by people who "get" it. We are connected because we are all taking action, not necessarily on the same issues or in the same way, but we are all activists in our own way. That's where I feel the most safe,

welcome, and understood. School, though, sometimes is a completely different story.

Oftentimes, when I return to school after travelling, I feel quite the opposite. I am often mocked and put down. A lot of this plays out because my peers see my posts on social media, and let's just say that what I post online is pretty different from what most teenagers post. And that's okay. I'm all for posting what you want, and I actually really like a lot of the stuff I see. But my friends aren't posting about kindness and how we can make the world a better place, you know? So I come back to school and hear questions such as, "Did you save the world yet, Hannah?" said in the most sarcastic tone.

By now you know that I am not a bystander, whether it is standing up for something I believe in on my blog or standing up for someone in the schoolyard. I do this instinctively; it's not a choice to me. It's who I am. When I see someone being bullied or I hear people using terms offensively, I call them on it. Using terms offensively, or accusing me of being something I am not, really hurts. It really stings. So, I've called people on it, and their response is always something like, "What are you going to do, Hannah, go write a blog post about it?" (Asked in the same sarcastic tone mentioned above.)

I could tell you that I brush it off. That they're just words. That I don't care what people think. But I'm not going to tell you that, because it's not true. I told you I was going to be honest and vulnerable—and so here I am.

I did write that blog post. I called it "Sticks and Stones May Break My Bones, But Words Will Last Forever." Because that's the truth. Every time I hear something negative said to me, about me or about my activism, it affects me. It lowers my self-esteem, and self-doubt kicks in. I've sometimes wondered if I've made the right choices. If maybe I'd have more friends or an easier time socially at school if I wasn't an activist.

Do you want to know how I deal with this? First, I give myself the opportunity to be affected by it. Sometimes that's 30 seconds, sometimes it's 30 minutes. But I don't stay in that place too long. I've learned to develop a thick skin and also perspective. As I said, I love what I do and believe in it. At the end of the day, I feel good.

I don't want to give you the impression I don't have friends. I do. I have friends both at school and beyond who are awesome. They are fun and supportive and always ready to hang out, go to concerts, or just talk. I'm really lucky that way, too.

There's another challenge with what I do—the travelling is amazing, and I'm out there doing things that are important to me,

but when I'm away from school, I miss things. My teachers have always been supportive and understanding, but they have never cut back on any projects, assignments, or tests. So when I'm away, I have to keep up and catch up on the work I miss. I have studied on planes, trains, and automobiles. Literally. I have worked on projects in airports, hotel rooms, and restaurants. When I was on the WE Create Change Tour from April to June, I had a teacher on the road and we worked for a set number of hours every day. Math has always been a struggle for me; I just don't think that way. The older I get, the more difficult it is to catch up on the instruction and class time that I miss in math. I have a math tutor twice a week, and meet with my teacher during recess and lunchtime. It's really stressful sometimes keeping on top of it all. School is important to me—my education is important to me.

The other consequence to missing as much school as I do is that I miss out on everyday things, such as clubs and student council. I love those things. I would really like to be more involved in my school community, but I've had to realize it's not fair to anyone when I can't make the time commitments. I know this because when I have been involved, I miss meetings since I'm away or because I need to spend the time with my math teacher. I know I've let people down when I couldn't be as available as they needed, and that was hard for everyone, especially me.

I've been thinking a lot about a conversation I once had with Spencer West when we were travelling. We were talking about how hard it is sometimes being away from home and missing those everyday things we used to take for granted. Life keeps moving forward whether you're there or not. You miss celebrating birthdays and holidays with friends and family. You miss going to movies and baseball games with your friends. Spencer told me about a time when he had just come back from a few weeks on the road and was at a cottage with a bunch of his friends, and there were moments that felt kind of awkward. He'd never felt that way before with them—they were his closest friends. But while he was away, they hadn't stopped hanging out together, and so they had a whole bunch of memories and inside jokes he wasn't in on.

That conversation with Spencer was a really important one for me, because I realized it's not just me—this life we've chosen, that we work hard for, that we believe in and love, is hard sometimes, for all of us.

I want to bring this full circle and come back to where I started. I love what I do. Being an activist, blogger, and motivational speaker is fulfilling and it's who I am. But I'd be lying if I said my life is always filled with sunshine and rainbows. Sometimes it's stressful to balance it all, and sometimes it makes me a target. I tell you this because I want you to know it's inevitable that you will have challenges on your journey. Can you think of one successful person who hasn't overcome challenges to get to where they are? None? Me, neither.

When you are in those moments when you're stressed out, misunderstood, or overwhelmed, STOP. Remember your why. Why did you start? Why do you do it? And then, keep going.

"COMPASSION IS NOT COMPASSION WITHOUT ACTION."

Vivienne Harr

VIVIENNE HARR:
PEACE ACTIVIST, ENTREPRENEUR

Vivienne Harr and I have a lot in common: we're about the same age; we both started our activism before we were 10 years old; and we both believe you are NEVER too young to understand that there are some really awful things happening in the world and that we can do something about them. I first learned about Vivienne when I was on the WE Create Change Tour. One night, on a bed in a hotel room somewhere between Calgary and Vancouver, my mom and I watched the doc #StandWithMe on our laptop.

In 2012, eight-year-old Vivienne sat down with a book by humanitarian photographer Lisa Kristine, who herself is creating change through photos that give social justice a face. This book sparked Vivienne's action; it was filled with photos of child labourers. One photo stood out: two young brothers from Nepal held hands as they carried huge cement blocks strapped to their backs.

Vivienne was shocked and saddened, but she wanted to turn her "compassion into action." She told her parents she wanted to free 500 children from child labour. How? A lemonade stand.

My issue is
children's rights.

Vivienne's goal was to raise $100,000. **After six months, she donated $101,320 to Not for Sale, an anti-slavery campaign.**

It's hard to imagine raising that much money with a lemonade stand,. right? I have many friends who have set up lemonade stands or organized car washes and bake sales for causes they cared about. Vivienne started out charging 50 cents per cup. Her plan was to set up her stand every single day for a year, but she soon realized that even if she did, she wouldn't reach her goal. So she changed her approach to "pay what's in your heart."

"People would ask why I was doing that. I'd say, 'It's by donation,' and they would ask, 'Oh really? What's it for?' And then I would tell them my story. That grabbed their attention, and they would always pay above and beyond. Sometimes I got $100 for a cup, which is amazing."

Soon the media were curious about what she was doing.

"People would see me as hope for the next generation. And seeing that kids could make a difference, and the fact that I was doing so much at such a young age, was really interesting to people. They would try to find out about me, and then that gave more publicity to my story and more awareness about child slavery."

Vivienne was passionate and determined, and raising awareness about child slavery was just as important to her as raising the money. I asked her what made her think she could make a difference at only eight years old.

"I've always felt that I had a voice, and I've always felt like I should use my voice for something good. I really always believed in myself, and I believed in what I was doing, and I was confident about my cause."

I had similar thoughts when I was starting out. I never said, "Oh, I'm just one person" or "No one is going to listen to me." I just went for it. So did Vivienne. We talked about the skeptics—those people who doubted what we were doing and questioned why we were doing it in the first place—and Vivienne shared this:

"People would say, 'Why don't you leave this to the professionals who have been doing this for a long time?' I would say, 'It's a cause that I've really been passionate about and I was tired of waiting around for someone to do something more.' I never stopped believing I could do it because I've always believed that I can do things."

❝ I've always felt that **I had a voice**, and I've always felt like **I should use my voice** for **something good**. **❞**

Vivienne Harr

45

My gift is Commitment.

Vivienne told me that her dad, mom, and younger brother have always been super supportive. I had the opportunity to talk to Vivienne's dad, Eric—he's amazing, and it was easy to see where Vivienne gets "it" from. I asked him what his reaction was when Vivienne declared she wanted to set up a lemonade stand to free 500 child labourers.

"I think at first the reaction of grown-ups is to think of all the reasons why you can't. We've sort of seen life and seen the things that don't work, and we become a little cynical. Kids aren't constrained in their thinking. You can dream big. You can dream of a world of peace, and we need you to push for that because we tend to see the obstacles."

Eric said Vivienne was so determined that "she led by example and we followed, and that's the message. She didn't just say it, she did it, and she kept doing it, and it rallied us, and then it rallied the neighbourhood, and then it rallied the world."

I asked Vivienne what day stands out as the most memorable for her. Out of 365 days, there had to be quite a few to choose from.

"When I brought my lemonade stand to Hawaii. We were going on a vacation for my dad's triathlon, so we brought it in a big box, bought the ingredients locally, and made the lemonade there. So, we did it in Hawaii and that was really fun."

I have met a lot of committed people over the years, but when Vivienne told me that, she blew my mind. That is next-level commitment!

Vivienne has written a children's book, spoken at the United Nations and the Vatican, met the Dalai Lama, and more (look her up online!). Her ultimate goal is to be the first U.S. Secretary of Peace.

"I think we need a position where someone's advocating for peace in whatever form that takes, whether it's a cause you believe in, such as no war or no animal abuse or no child abuse. There should be someone who is supporting you, and someone in the government who is advocating for peace."

The change is working toward peace.

WE CREATE CHANGE

In the fall of 2012, I started learning more and more about Free The Children (now called the WE Movement) and discovered there were hundreds of thousands of young people who were passionate about the same things I was and were taking action on them. Knowing there was a huge community out there that offered support and resources, I was motivated to learn more.

That year, the issue that WE was highlighting was access to clean water, and that was my entry point into global issues. It was also when I first started to see myself as a global citizen. Through WE Villages, WE works in developing communities in eight countries through their five pillars of impact: Education, Water, Health, Food, and Opportunity. Each pillar is a critical component in breaking the cycle of poverty, and they all work together because each one affects the other.

Something we forget or don't know is that in developing communities, clean water is not a given. Girls my age walk for hours to fill jugs of water from the river. The river is their source of water for everything—bathing, laundry, and cooking. It's worth mentioning that animals walk through the river, and some even live in it. You can imagine that this water, which is brown and dirty, is contaminated. Many people become sick or contract fatal diseases by drinking it. But for many people it is the only water source, and we all need water to live.

So, back to the girls. Since they are mostly the ones responsible for collecting the water for their families, and it often takes hours

and hours every day, there isn't always an opportunity for them to go to school. This is an example of how the WE pillars are connected; in this case, Water, Health, and Education. There are many reasons that girls don't go to school—collecting water for several hours a day and getting sick because the water is dirty are two of them. Making clean, safe water accessible removes these barriers to going to school.

In 2012, WE had just launched WE Create Change, a campaign to raise awareness and funds to provide access to clean water. It was the year that Canada was saying goodbye to the penny, and WE Create Change was all about collecting pennies. Every $25 collected would provide clean water to one person for life. WE Create Change was a way I believed I could truly make a difference.

I was in Grade 4 and I had just started my blog. I talked to my principal and told her what I wanted to do, and she was excited to get the school involved. We made our plans to launch WE Create Change at our upcoming assembly, and I offered to speak. It was the first time I got on stage.

I didn't know it at the time, but that speech was a bunch of milestone moments for me. It was the first time I realized I could motivate and mobilize my peers and my community to make a difference. It was also the first time I saw myself as a leader. It was the first time I saw that one of my gifts was public speaking and that I could use my voice to create change.

I was awed by the response of my school. We spent the next month collecting pennies, and it was incredible. My teachers and friends were eager to act, and amazing things started to happen. It was motivating and unifying to know that every penny we collected wasn't just making a difference in another country, it was making a difference in our school community, too. Students who would never have spent time together were working together to get this done. In working toward a common goal, we found that our differences became less important and we, as a school community, became stronger.

At the end of the month, my friends and I gathered to sort, count, and bag the coins. In one month, between two schools, we had collected over 97,500 pennies, enough to provide clean water for 37 people for life.

Four years later, I travelled to Kenya and had a full-circle moment when I did the water walk with Mama Jane.

The water walk is a part of every ME to WE trip. It's about fully experiencing why access to clean water is so urgent. Mama Jane and her daughter Mama Judy and I walked from their home down to the Mara River. I saw for myself the brown and dirty water we made our way to collect. Mama Judy helped me fill my jug, and she showed me how to carry it on my head. The jug of water weighed almost 10 kg (22 lb). It would have been 23 kg (50 lb) if I'd been an adult. We made the long walk back to Mama Jane's home. Many girls and mamas do this walk five times a day to get the water they need.

After dropping off our water jugs, we walked a very short distance and filled new jugs with clean water from the wells—one of the wells that my classmates and I had collected all those pennies for.

It all adds up. Every penny and every student. That's what I was thinking about while standing there with Mama Jane.

"CARPE DIEM."

Blake Mycoskie

BLAKE MYCOSKIE:
FOUNDER & CHIEF SHOE GIVER OF TOMS

The inspiration for TOMS came to Blake Mycoskie while vacationing in Argentina in 2006. He noticed that many children he saw there didn't have shoes. That sparked his idea to create a business with a simple concept: buy a new pair of shoes and give one new pair of shoes. Ten years later, TOMS has given 70 million pairs of shoes to kids in need.

The One for One model has grown to include other products and other gives. Eyeglasses, coffee, purses, and backpacks help give sight, clean water, health care for safe childbirth, and support for anti-bullying programs. TOMS partners with over 100 organizations to make a difference in 93 countries.

Fun fact: There isn't a guy named Tom who has anything to do with TOMS. TOMS comes from the word "tomorrow" and the idea that we can create a better tomorrow. I'm all for that. You, too, right?

TOMS began with a small idea that grew to big change. I've been wearing TOMS and following Blake on social media for as long as I can remember and was excited to talk to him from his home in Los Angeles.

If there is one thing that has been consistent in my journey, it is role models, so whenever I get a chance to ask some of my role models who their role models are, I always take it. Clearly, Blake thinks a lot about role models, too.

"As I was thinking about my business and growing it, I read a lot of biographies of other successful business owners who I felt had done interesting and different things."

We talked about how much there is to learn from those who have been on the path that we want to go on. For me, it was Severn, Marc, and Craig who inspired me, because they all began their own journeys at such a young age.

Blake named Yvon Chouinard (founder of Patagonia, a clothing and gear company), Howard Schultz (Starbucks), and Richard Branson (Virgin Group) as role models. He said that from each of their stories he took away something that inspired him. They all contributed to Blake's mindset of creating a business that has social impact and of not being afraid to take risks.

When Blake came up with the One for One model, he told me that people said things such as "That seems like a really risky idea" or "I don't know if that'll work."

Reading books by and about his role models gave Blake the confidence to be bold and creative.

My issue is improving lives through business.

"I'm really thankful that I was able to read some of these books and do some of this work early on because that's what gave me the confidence."

When I asked him about his advice to young people, he said the following:

"Read as much as you can about people who have done something similar to what you want to do. Interviewing them is great, such as what you're doing right now. That's kind of how I had role models, mainly through the books I read about other entrepreneurs."

This is really something that I believe in, and I say this all the time: identify those people who prove that it—whatever your "it" is—can be done. My bookshelf is evidence of this.

Blake said something really interesting when I asked him if he has met the role models from his bookshelf.

"You don't necessarily have to meet them. Just hearing their stories can motivate you to be kind of the best that you can be, and I think that's really important when you think about what you're trying to do as you go forward."

My gift is the ability to see opportunities that others don't.

In your own journey, you will find role models that you'll never meet. I have. I won't meet Princess Diana, Nelson Mandela, or Martin Luther King Jr., because they have passed away. And some role models are fictional characters, like Auggie in *Wonder*. But I will always be inspired by their life and message when I read their stories.

I told Blake about Issue + Gift = Change, and he reflected on the very beginning of TOMS (before it had become TOMS) and pinpointed the moment he discovered his issue: these kids, they don't have shoes. He explained that important ideas and revelations can come to you when you are relaxed or open to them.

"A big idea like TOMS starts as kind of a small hunch or intuition, and I think that happens when you're in situations where you're relaxed. For me, it happens a lot when I'm in nature. I was very relaxed. I was enjoying myself. I was curious. All those things led to me being kind of open enough to have an idea like TOMS, and also open enough to kind of experiment with it and see what it could be."

Blake added that getting out of the office and into a new environment is important. Being somewhere different allows you to tap into creativity. Being out there in the world and really seeing, listening, and hearing about other people's lives will uncover issues that you didn't realize mattered to you.

One of the things that I've been asked since I was 10 years old is "What are you going to be when you grow up?" At 14, I'm still figuring that out. I have some ideas; journalism really excites me right now. What I do know for sure, though, is that whatever career path I take, it's going to involve social good. Because Blake is such a successful businessman and global change-maker, I asked him to share his career advice for young people or businesses that want to make a difference.

"The piece of advice I give to young people more and more is really to follow your passion and to not just do something for the money. Because at the end of the day, it's your passion that will enable you to make a difference."

And there you have it. Passion. We should all be as lucky as Blake, to be able to build our passion into our life's work and make a difference every day.

The change is organizing people around an idea.

HANNAH'S REFLECTION ON CONSCIOUS CONSUMERISM

Blake said something really important during our conversation that I'd like to mention now. He said, "How you spend your money is how you show your values, and if you're supporting businesses that are aligned with your values, you'll feel better about how you spend your money." This is a really big deal, and it's also a way you can take action every single day.

What Blake is talking about is how to be a conscious consumer—that is, someone who thinks about how and what they purchase and use. Conscious consumerism is about making the best possible choices, whether for people or the environment or, in the best-case scenario, both.

We are big consumers, and it's probably fair to say we consume things almost all day every day. When I think about it like that, I'm including everything from the electricity in our homes to the gas in our cars, plus our food, drink, clothes, and entertainment. It's really everything we use, right?

Now, if you're like me, you're likely not the one in your family actually spending the money and making the decisions about what items you're going to buy and where you're going to buy them. But that doesn't mean you can't help make those choices and influence those decisions. A big part of taking action is doing research and sharing your knowledge so you can influence others.

Below are some ideas on how to, as Blake says, "show your values."

Shop Local

When you buy products that are made and food that is grown locally, there are several positive impacts. By purchasing from local businesses and farmers, you are supporting the local economy, which means the sellers can provide for their families. When we're talking specifically about fruits and vegetables, they are fresher because they don't need to be shipped a long way to get to you. Bonus: less transporting is also better for the environment.

Buy Fair Trade

The fair trade movement considers everything involved in the product, including how something is made and who is making it. These are really important things to think about, as they bring the human side to a buying decision. Are the people who played a part in making the product being paid fairly? Are their working conditions safe? Is the production of this product safe for the environment? While products that are fair trade are sometimes more expensive, it's worth looking at all of the costs to make them, including the human and environmental costs.

Look for Eco-friendly Products

Look for less packaging, products that are either made from recycled material or material that can be recycled, and also products that will last a long time so they don't need to be replaced (a.k.a. repurchased) where possible. Thinking about eco-friendly products also includes reusing things like water bottles and shopping bags. The fewer things we need to throw out, the better. It's worth noting that of the three Rs—reduce, reuse, recycle—the first two are the most important. Recycling is better than sending stuff to the landfill, but it still does take a lot of energy to recycle.

Favour Companies and Products that Give

Look for the products and companies that share your values and have giving built into their business model. It's probably obvious that TOMS is one of these companies. Blake's whole concept for TOMS is based on the idea that "if someone can afford to buy a pair, then they would feel great giving a pair." Over the last few years, TOMS has added other products, such as bags, sunglasses, and coffee, so the company can give in other ways (funding clean water, safe births, and anti-bullying programs).

The ME to WE collection of products is created by members of the communities where WE works. Each product supports one of the five pillars of impact of their work in WE Villages: Education, Water, Health, Food, and Opportunity. Each product also comes with Track Your Impact, a unique code you can enter online to see exactly where and how you are making a difference with your purchase.

Roxanne Joyal, CEO and co-founder of ME to WE, says her favourite thing about the ME to WE Artisans program is that it has enabled more than 1,500 mamas in Kenya to provide their children with education. When I was in Kenya, I spent time with the mamas beading and talking about how their lives have been impacted by having the opportunity to create and sell their jewellery.

Maybe now is a good time to point out that many of the values mentioned above were taken into consideration when creating this book. For one, it's printed on Rolland Enviro Print Paper—check out the box on this page for cool facts about this paper. Also, a portion of the sale of every book is being donated to WE in support of the work they do locally and globally through WE Charity. And that doesn't even begin to include all the awesome change that is going to come out of what you're inspired to do. Right? High-fives all around.

Using one ton of Rolland Enviro Print Paper instead of a virgin paper saves the equivalent of

- 17 trees
- 761 kg (1,678 lb) of solid waste
- 63,000 litres (16,399 gallons) of water
- 2,500 kg (5,512 lb) of greenhouse gas emissions

Blake Mycoskie

"WORK HARD AND BE NICE TO PEOPLE."

Lilly Singh

LILLY SINGH:
YOUTUBE CREATOR, AUTHOR, COMEDIAN, ROLE MODEL, BAWSE

Lilly Singh, a.k.a. Superwoman, is slaying the world through social media. Over 12 million people subscribe to her YouTube channel, and her videos have been viewed over ONE BILLION TIMES. (I might be responsible for many of those views.)

In 2017, Lilly became a New York Times *bestselling author with her book* How to Be a BAWSE. *For Lilly, it's all about how we can hustle harder, let go of our FOMO (fear of missing out), and be unapologetically ourselves.*

Lilly inspires me because she believes we can be better and more compassionate, and I admire her so much for her attitude and message. She doesn't have millions of YouTube views and millions of fans around the world just because she's hilarious and makes people laugh (although she is and she does)—it's also because she makes people think and take steps to be the best that they can be.

We both believe that we can create the greatest change when we support each other. Lilly launched #GirlLove, a social media campaign to combat girl-on-girl hate. It promotes her belief that amazing things happen when girls lift each other up.

My issue is
women's issues.

Lilly made her first YouTube video in 2010 when she wasn't happy. She was watching YouTube videos and feeling sad and lonely— like she didn't belong anywhere.

"Because I was a sad person at that time and wanted to make myself laugh and do something as a creative project, I decided to post a video, thinking nothing of it. I didn't think I would post another one, and I definitely didn't think it would be my career. I just posted a video and it was really bad. Seventy people watched it, and I fell in love with the idea of being creative on my own terms."

Something Lilly and I have in common is that we both genuinely have the best time doing what we love. Lilly was really sad before she found this creative space to use her voice, and now she's helping others learn about how they can find their own voices and be happy doing what they love.

One of the things that shines through Lilly's videos is her passion, especially when it comes to #GirlLove. Lilly told me that the mission of #GirlLove is to promote the idea, especially among young girls, that it's cool to support each other instead of participating in girl-on-girl hate.

"The way media portray women, it's very easy for young girls to think it's cool and normal and expected to dislike other girls and not work together. I want to change that. I want young girls to grow up knowing it's actually really cool to support other women, and it's important because there are so many causes around the

world that, unfortunately, negatively impact women, and the only way to really tackle those is if women are not competing against each other. It's the belief that if we come together as women, we can tackle such issues worldwide."

#GirlLove is extremely important. I see girl-on-girl hate happening everywhere, and I'd love to see it end, too. So, if there's anything I can do to support #GirlLove, I am all over it.

Lilly said she originally didn't set out for #GirlLove to become a movement. "It started with me making a challenge video, where I got my friends to make videos complimenting other women, and I thought, 'Okay. It's just a new video. It's done. It's over.' But then it really sparked something within me, and because it was so well received, I decided to make #GirlLove a thing. I now have a complete social media strategy and team for it."

My gift is my Social platform.

Lilly is such a positive person. Some days, it's hard to be positive. I asked her how she does it.

"One of the things that helps me stay positive is to be grateful. I think when you start to open your eyes to everything you actually do have, that's when you start to be positive. If you focus on every small thing that's going wrong in a day, you're never going to be able to be positive. For example, a lot of things went wrong today, but then I thought, 'All right, I have an amazing career. It's sunny outside! I have a car! I'm talking to Hannah! This is all good stuff!' So I think it's focusing on all the [positive] things and actually calling them out when you're experiencing them."

So that's how she does it.

I asked her what it means to be a "bawse."

"A bawse is someone who not only conquers in the workplace but does what they can to be the best version of themselves in their professional life, their personal life, and their relationships, and how they communicate and how self-aware they are. It is someone who doesn't just survive life but conquers life in the best way possible."

For someone my age, when Lilly talks about conquering in the workplace, that means school—and, really, wherever and however we spend our time.

RAPID FIRE WITH LILLY

HANNAH: What's your favourite video you've ever filmed?

LILLY: Oooooooh, it's going to be the one with Selena Gomez. And not just because it's Selena, but you know when you really look up to someone and then you meet them and they're so wonderful? That's what my experience was with her. She's everything and more that I wanted her to be.

What's your most prized possession?

I have this pillow, and its name is KFEMZ! My mom made it for me and it travels with me around the world for every tour, everywhere I go, and I'm hugging it right now!

If YouTube didn't exist, what would you be doing?

Probably something related to psychology because that's what I have a degree in. So, probably a counsellor of some sort.

Who are five of your Girl Loves?

Definitely Beyoncé, definitely Selena Gomez, definitely Michelle Obama, my mom, and ... I'm going to say ... Alicia Keys.

What does being a unicorn mean to you?

Being a unicorn means you care about and value being a good, warm, kind-hearted person. Even though people say unicorns are mythical, I don't believe it. I think a little unicorn spirit can live in all of us, and that means you actively care about being nice and being kind.

HANNAH'S REFLECTION

CHANGE: IT HAS TO START SOMEWHERE

Lilly was in Kenya with ME to WE in the summer of 2016 just a few weeks after I was. Like me, she was visiting for the first time. I followed her posts on social media about the trip, and I couldn't wait to see her vlog on YouTube. It was cool because she and I had very similar itineraries, experiences, and feelings about what we discovered during our time with the community in the Maasai Mara.

When I asked Lilly to share her advice for young people who want to make a difference, she wanted to share something that she herself learned in Kenya.

"Something I've learned through working with WE, and it was a huge eye-opener when I went to Kenya, was that so often, you

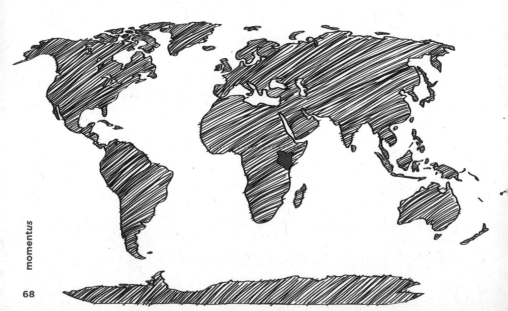

think problems are so big that we can't help them. Prior to going to Kenya, I remember having conversations with people and they would say, 'What's that really going to change? What could [you] be doing that will really make a change, and how is that really going to help people?' Then I got to Kenya and I saw in that community all the wells that were built, and the simple solutions of a girl being able to go to school because the well was at school so they don't have to go and fetch water. It was such a simple solution, and all it took was someone to do it, someone to put effort toward it. So I just want to say any effort you put toward anything, and any small change it makes, is still progress. No problem is too big to fix if you start fixing it."

Exactly. This is what I saw and felt in Kenya, too. It's a huge myth that the issues we see are just so big—maybe even too big.

It can be overwhelming, and sometimes so much so that it stops people from doing something. So starting might be the hardest part. But let me tell you, once you start, it's even harder to stop. It is the most amazing thing to see real, tangible change, and it draws you in and makes you want to be part of it.

In 2013, I created a pledge for Earth Day: "**Stop. Start. Continue.**" I think of Earth Day kind of like New Year's Day, but for the Earth, and the pledge was like the yearly resolutions many of us make. It was about making eco-friendly commitments to **stop** doing things that were harmful to the environment, **start** doing something that would have a positive impact, and **continue** doing the things you were already doing to make a difference. The **continue** part was really important because it's about recognizing that you're already doing something to make a difference.

I launched the pledge on my blog with a certificate you could download and print, and then fill in your pledge. I also shared it on social media, asking people to join me and make their own "**Stop. Start. Continue.**" pledge. It didn't take long before I was getting responses on social media, and the comments on my blog posts filled with what people were pledging to do. Something really cool that happened is that some teachers told me they had made copies of the pledge for their class. They were using it for their Earth Day activity, and every student was making their own pledge to make a difference.

In 2014, I launched the pledge for a second year, and this time I added a certificate for families. I was so aware that the change I was creating was being supported by my parents, and that many of the eco-friendly things I was doing were things we were committing to as a family.

I made the printable certificates in black and white with lots of items to colour. The hope was that families would post them on their fridge as a reminder of the resolution and commitment they had made. It was like saying, "Remember! You have to do this!"

The picture above is the pledge I made on Earth Day 2014. I committed to **stop** leaving the lights on when I leave a room, **start** an eco team at camp, and **continue** using my voice to make a difference. It has been on my fridge ever since.

Change must start somewhere, which sometimes means stopping something that's not working, and in order for a change to stick, you have to continue doing what you know makes a difference.

 So, what will your "**Stop. Start. Continue.**" pledge be?

"I AM ONLY ONE, BUT I AM ONE.
I CANNOT DO EVERYTHING, BUT
I CAN DO SOMETHING. AND I
WILL NOT LET WHAT I CANNOT
DO INTERFERE WITH WHAT
I CAN DO."

Travis Price,
quoting author
Edward
Everett Hale

TRAVIS PRICE:
ANTI-BULLYING ADVOCATE,
CO-FOUNDER OF PINK SHIRT DAY

From supporting one bullied teenager in Nova Scotia to supporting and educating youth around the world, Travis Price is what you might call an everyday hero. On the first day of Grade 12 in 2007, Travis and his friend DJ witnessed a Grade 9 student being tormented and bullied at school. They hated that this was happening and decided to do something. Enough was enough. It was clear the student had become a target based on what he was wearing—a pink T-shirt.

After school, Travis and DJ bought 50 pink shirts and then emailed everyone they knew. They wrote, "Tomorrow we are creating a Sea of Pink. Wear pink to stand with this boy. Wear pink to stand up to the boys who bullied him. When we stand together wearing pink, the bullies will be forced to step down." The next morning, hundreds of students showed up in pink shirts. When that Grade 9 student walked in and saw his peers in pink, he smiled and sighed. He was not alone.

That day, the movement now called Pink Shirt Day was born.

My issue is ensuring everyone has access to bullying prevention education.

Travis is pretty special to me. We became friends when we both spoke on the 2014/2015 WE Day Tour. His story shows that sometimes the biggest change comes from small acts. Everyone can do something for someone at some time. Travis and I caught up via Skype in the middle of his Pink Shirt Day Tour. I asked him if he ever thought his actions 10 years ago would make such a huge difference for so many people.

"We never thought it would be anything, so there was never a fear of it not working or people latching on. We just wanted to show that kid it was okay. We actually thought we might get beat up. We thought we might be the only two in pink, and we were kind of ready for that. If it went down that way, it went down. But we would be able to know that we stood up for him."

But that's not what happened. Ten years later, the pink shirt is a symbol against bullying all over the world. Pink Shirt Day is a day where we come together, creating a sea of pink. It's a day that empowers us to stand up against bullying because we do it together.

"I think we not only made a difference to that boy, but we changed the culture within our school to the point we're now changing the culture around the world and the way people are addressing bullying."

Today Travis is an anti-bullying advocate. It's his full-time job. I wanted to know if the way he talks about bullying has changed since 2007.

"My message has varied slightly, based on what I've learned and how important it is that we talk about bullying in a certain way. We don't address people as bullies; we say they are people who bully, because bullying is simply behaviour, and behaviours can change. But if we label somebody a bully, that means that's who they are, that's what they need to be, and people try to live up to expectations, people try to live up to those labels, unfortunately."

The same goes for the person being bullied. We shouldn't label people who are bullied as victims, and they don't need to define themselves that way. We need to isolate the experience.

"But my message is still the same: that one person can make a difference, one person can save somebody, and we need to continue to talk about bullying openly and freely, and not be scared to address the issues that happen to us."

My gift is being able to relate to youth affected by bullying.

Travis Price

This is really the idea behind Pink Shirt Day—keeping the conversation about bullying active and letting everyone know they have allies and people to turn to. It's as simple as going up to someone and saying, "I'm here for you and am ready to listen to you." Having an open ear reminds people they are not alone and they have people who support them.

I post about Pink Shirt Day on my social media accounts. Sometimes the day gets criticized or receives comments, such as "Why is Pink Shirt Day one day? Why can't we talk about bullying every day?" I asked Travis what he says to people when he gets these questions.

"I say the goal is to make Pink Shirt Day every day, but that's not up to me. That's up to them. It's up to teachers, and it's up to community leaders to make the choice that they will address bullying in their schools, in their communities. That's the only way. Research shows that bullying prevention education is great for schools. When we educate youth to deliver the message to other youth, that's when we see our strongest results."

Travis believes that once every student, teacher, and community leader steps up and says "enough is enough" that's when we'll make every day Pink Shirt Day. Everyone needs to help make bullying stop.

The change is helping to end bullying.

It can be hard, though, to stand up for what you believe in or stand up for others you see being bullied. Travis gave me some good advice on what we can do if we find ourselves in that situation.

"If you see someone being bullied online, or face to face, it doesn't necessarily mean you have to step up for that person in that moment and shut those kids down. You can go and get a teacher. That can be just as helpful as standing up directly."

I share Travis's story as often as I can when I'm speaking to groups of students and educators. For me, it really is one of the best examples I've come across that shows how what seem like the smallest things can make the biggest difference. As Travis says, "It's the little acts, the simple acts of kindness that can make the world of difference. We never set out to change the world; we just set out to help somebody."

" If you see someone being **bullied** online, or face to face, **it doesn't necessarily** mean you have to step up for that person **in that moment** and shut those kids down. **You can go and get a teacher.** That can be **just as helpful** as **standing up directly**. **"**

Travis Price

77

THE POWER OF SOCIAL MEDIA

People call my generation "digital natives." What they mean is that Internet technology has always been part of our everyday lives. It's hard to imagine life without it, right? So it's natural that I would use it as a tool and a resource to connect and to share. When I post on my blog or social media platforms, my voice is amplified and so are my connections to like-minded youth all over the world. Over the years, I have connected with so many awesome people and organizations that are taking action on all kinds of issues. With social media, you don't need a stage or an audience to be heard. You can reach people online everywhere and anywhere.

I use my blog and my social media platforms—Twitter, Instagram, Facebook, Snapchat—to share the good. I post motivational quotes that I love, kind reminders that people are awesome, stories that inspire me, and information about events I'm attending and what they stand for. I follow and share posts from people and organizations that are doing the same thing. The "social" in social media is what makes it powerful as a connector. It has become a way to connect, mobilize, share, and amplify.

Social media gives us the opportunity to connect globally and take action. A great example of this was the Women's March in January 2017. It began with an idea by a small group of women that, within days, became a call to action that led other groups of women around the world to organize marches on the same day.

POWER
TO THE
GIRLS

#WhyI March!

WOMEN'S
MARCH
—ON WASHINGTON—
TORONTO
QUEEN'S PARK

I went to the march in Toronto, and it was incredible to be a part of something locally while at the same time watching on social media as hundreds of thousands of people around the world took part in marches in their own communities.

There are tons of organizations out there that give you the opportunity to use social media for social good. For example, I love the organization Do Something. It's a global movement for good, taking action on a variety of different issues like the environment, homelessness, texting while driving, and more. There are hundreds of campaigns with different time commitments. All the initiatives have a social media aspect, whether it's posting a picture of you doing a challenge or motivating others. It's a way to help shift the culture of hate and revolutionize how we use the Internet—for good.

So the "social" in social media can be awesome. But like all things that are "social," it's not always sunshine and rainbows. Travis and I talked about this fact, too, because in his work as an anti-bullying activist, he has seen how social media has changed the issue of bullying. He said, "When I was being bullied as a kid it was until three o'clock. I'd leave school and go home, and home was safe. Now, kids go home, and at three-fifteen the phone buzzes and kids see stuff online. It's twenty-four/seven." When the bullying turns into cyberbullying, you can't get away from it. For some kids, it doesn't stop.

Many in my generation are constantly online, so the bullying IRL (in real life) follows us wherever we go, making it hard—or impossible—to shut out. According to PREVNet (a network of 130 Canadian research scientists and 62 national youth-serving organizations), one in three Canadian youth reports they have been cyberbullied. FYI, the term "cyberbullying" was officially added to the *Oxford English Dictionary* in 2011.

And what happens on social media doesn't stay on social media. Social media posts—the ones we make and the ones we see—have effects that are life-changing. Many students who are cyberbullied often feel alone and scared, and don't want to go to school. They may become depressed and withdrawn. Tragically, some young people have taken their own lives. The people doing the cyberbullying may be suspended from school, lose their jobs, and even be charged. Social media is a powerful tool. Used responsibly, it can change the world for the better. Used irresponsibly, it can damage lives forever.

Too many youth my age measure their worth in "likes" and "followers." According to one survey, teens delete about half the photos in their Instagram feed because they didn't get enough "likes." But let me tell you something: the only "like" and "follower" that matters is your own.

Now, about some of those photos we see on social media— the ones on some of the most followed accounts of celebrities and "influencers." Those photos that look effortless and natural are sometimes the ones that have the most effort put into them. Many of the photos we see are no less styled or produced than a magazine photo shoot. It might also be fair to say that many of us take dozens of shots to get the "right" one to post and share. Not to mention photo editing and filters. I'm not saying there's anything wrong with this. I do it, too. Our phones give us the opportunity, so why not, right? What I am saying, though, is that we need to recognize that what we see on social media is not always what it appears to be.

Travis Price

When I started blogging, I was nine years old and far too young to have any social media accounts. You must be 13 for most of them, and while many people often lie about their age in order to sign up for accounts, it's not something I did. So my social media experience grew out of my experience blogging, and it has really guided not only what I do and share on social media but how I do it. A lot of work goes into writing a blog post—sometimes it takes hours and sometimes days to get it right. I create an outline (sometimes on paper and sometimes in my head), and then I write, edit, choose photos, edit photos, create graphics, tag, categorize, and then review and edit one more time before I hit "Publish." I really do a lot of that for social media, too. Before I hit the "Tweet" or "Share" button, I review to make sure that I'm saying what I want to say. I do social media in the same way I blog, and for me, these platforms are really like mini-blogs. And just like my blog, my social media accounts are a history of me.

Below are some tips based on my own experiences that guide me on social media:

1. Do not engage with the negative comments. Do not feed the trolls.
2. Delete. (Some platforms allow you to delete comments in your feed. Where you can control what is on your wall, do it. Like graffiti, you can remove it if it's not welcome.)
3. Block. (If people are bothering or harassing you, block them.)
4. Do not click "Like" if you don't actually like it.
5. Do respond to the positive. Be the good kind of "social" in social media.
6. Do be positive. Share good things—videos, photos, quotes, stories.
7. Curate your feed. Fill it with what fills you.
8. If you feel like you really need to respond to something negative, do it with class and positivity.
9. Think before you post. Take a minute before you hit the button.
10. Put it down. Go for a walk. Live IRL.
11. Be social media savvy. Remember, not everything is as it appears.
12. Passwords are private.
13. Try not to get caught up in the number of "likes" a post or photo gets.
14. Don't post or share anything (even via text or DM) you don't want broadcast.
15. Don't say things online you wouldn't say in public.
16. Don't post when you're really angry or really emotional.
17. Don't use social media to work through something—it's not a journal or a one-on-one conversation with a close friend.
18. It's not too early to think about your digital footprint.
19. Take your online presence seriously.
20. Remember, social media IS public.

"DON'T EVER STOP WRITING YOUR STORY, BECAUSE YOU NEVER KNOW IF YOUR STORY IS INSPIRING OTHERS TO WRITE THEIR STORY."

Shania Pruden

SHANIA PRUDEN:
YOUTH ACTIVIST, BLOGGER, SPEAKER, VOLUNTEER

Shania Pruden writes and speaks about Indigenous rights, mental health, and women's rights. I met Shania a few years ago at WE Day in Winnipeg, Manitoba. We hit it off and have been connected on social media ever since. What I admire most about Shania is her never-give-up attitude. When she was a young girl, people told her she would never get far in life because she was Indigenous and living in poverty. At first she believed them, but then she vowed to not let others decide her future. She would become the person SHE wanted to be.

Shania believes—like me—that you don't need to have a lot of money to make a difference in your community. She started volunteering when she was 10 years old and blogging at 15. I know why I started blogging and was curious to find out her reason. She said she was influenced by a friend who said blogging made her happy.

"I started writing about Indigenous issues in Canada," Shania told me, "but I didn't write just about the issues—I also wrote about ways we could solve them."

My issues are mental health, women's rights, and Indigenous issues.

I asked Shania why she was so passionate about Indigenous issues, and she said they really hit home for her. It's personal.

"The majority of our homeless people in Winnipeg are Indigenous, as are the majority of children and youth living in poverty. Most of the missing or murdered women in Winnipeg are Indigenous. It's not a topic that's talked about."

Another subject close to her heart is residential schools. And I'll be honest—I had never heard of residential schools until this year. I was shocked and angry when I learned about them. How had I not known? Shania told me her mom and grandparents had attended residential schools.

In Canada, more than 150,000 Indigenous children were separated from their families and communities and put in residential schools. They weren't allowed to speak their language or practise their culture.

"My mom went to a day school, so she wasn't forced to sleep away from her family. But many of my friends' parents or grandparents were taken away from their families at a young age."

I can't imagine being stripped away from my family and culture.

"The adult figures in their lives weren't very nice people, and it affected how they raised their children and then their children raised their children. It's a pattern. My grandparents don't really talk about it, and I don't expect them to talk about it, because it was a very tragic thing that happened."

I had so many questions for Shania. I had been trying to fully understand the history of residential schools and the idea of truth and reconciliation. I was grateful to be able to talk openly with Shania without judgment and even more grateful that she was able to talk openly with me. I wanted to hear Shania's views.

"People usually talk about the reconciliation part, but not the truth. The truth part of it is the stories of what actually happened to Indigenous people in residential schools. For me, truth and reconciliation means talking about it and then trying to work together to reconcile in a space where everyone's welcome."

I've been wanting to take action on truth and reconciliation, so I asked Shania what she thought about adding a land acknowledgement to the morning announcements at my school, right after the national anthem. A land acknowledgement shows recognition of and respect for Indigenous people and their history.

Shania had this to say:

"When I do my speeches, I always acknowledge that we're on treaty territory. I think it's really cool to acknowledge the land you're on and where it came from. Every time I hear a non-Indigenous person acknowledge the treaty land they're on, I have a lot of respect for them."

At many events I've been at lately, they've done this, and it feels right.

My gifts are my ability to connect with people and the courage to combat any negative obstacles that get in the way.

Something I have always loved about Shania is the inspiring and positive presence she has on social media. It's where she and I connect and where we both connect to our communities. We also both use social media to amplify what we're doing on our blogs and through our speaking engagements. It takes our voices to a different and larger audience. I asked her what she thinks about when she is ready to post something on social media.

"I make sure that everything I post is either an uplifting quote or something I really like. Or I share a story to motivate other people to share their stories. That's how you can use social media to help make a difference."

Social media for social good is something Shania and I both truly believe in. When we spread positive things and raise awareness about issues we care about on social media, they can reach people around the world. Shania and I found each other through social media because we are both change-makers and we have similar interests.

I always love to hear about the role models that people have, especially people like Shania who are so confident and work so hard to make a difference. I love hearing about the people who have played a part in guiding their journey. Shania told me she has two role models.

"My mom demonstrates strength in many ways. All of the positive and negative experiences she's been through have shaped me to be the person I am today. If she could survive these things, then so can I. My second role model is a politician named Nahanni Fontaine. She is the kind of politician I want to be one day. She had a very rough upbringing, but didn't let it stop her from enjoying life and making a difference. All of her community involvement definitely inspires me to continue with my community involvement."

The change is educating people about the truth.

YOUR COMMUNITY NEEDS YOU

One of the things that has always stood out for me about Shania is that she's really engaged in her community through volunteering. Giving a hand to local people and organizations is a great way to take action and check off a whole bunch of things that many of us have on our to-do lists, such as

- ☑ meet like-minded people
- ☑ make a tangible impact
- ☑ spend time with family and/or friends
- ☑ use your gift

In my mind, volunteering means anything from helping with a neighbourhood cleanup to spending time at a local food bank, from packing up boxes of donations for a shelter to helping a neighbour. To me, volunteering is giving of yourself. When you understand volunteering this way, you don't need to look too far in front of you or think too far ahead to make a difference.

I come from a long line of volunteers. My great-grandmother used to volunteer at her local seniors residence. She used to say she was "helping the old people." I should tell you that she said this when she herself was 85 years old. Since my grandparents have retired, they have each spent a few days a week volunteering at that same seniors residence.

Something I've come to understand about volunteering is that you can't be too old (as my great-grandmother proved), but

momentus

you *can* be too young. There was a time I spent hours and hours online looking for places where I could volunteer and discovered that at 13 years old, I was too young for many of the opportunities I found, which often had a minimum age of 16 or 18. By now you know that I'm open-minded and resourceful, and that I don't let something like my age stop me. There are lots of ways to give back, and I've found—and created—quite a few.

The Great Canadian Shoreline Cleanup

One of my very first actions was volunteering as a team leader for the Great Canadian Shoreline Cleanup, an initiative that engages communities across Canada to clean up their local water sources. On their website, they listed all the areas they were targeting, and I noticed no one had stepped up to organize a team in my neighbourhood. I signed up and shared with my friends and family the date, time, meeting place, and space we were responsible for. After a few hours and a whole lot of dirty gloves and boots, we had filled 10 huge bags of litter and trash that had been a big problem for the wildlife living in and near our creeks and streams. Mission accomplished.

Daily Bread Food Bank

After participating in and donating to many food drives, I wanted to volunteer at a local food bank and be part of the next steps to provide people in our community with the food they need. When I learned I was too young to go on my own, my dad volunteered to go with me. We spent a full day sorting food and getting it ready to hit the shelves in the distribution centre. Volunteering with family or friends is a great way to spend time together and do something meaningful. This is the win-win stuff.

#FeedTO

I wanted to do something to support people who were experiencing homelessness in downtown Toronto, but I was too young to volunteer at a shelter or soup kitchen. I came up with the idea for #FeedTO, and with the support of a friend of my dad's who has a food truck, we drove around in the morning and handed out fresh, hot meals. In the afternoon, we parked the food truck in a busy business area and hosted a "pay what you can" lunch, and we donated all the proceeds to the local food bank. Don't be afraid to get the people around you involved.

JUST GIVE

Sometimes volunteering can mean showing up. For me, JUST GIVE is just that. JUST GIVE is an initiative encouraging good deeds and kindness throughout the city. One of my favourite parts of the week-long campaign is holding doors open and giving high-fives to busy commuters at downtown Toronto's highest-traffic subway station. JUST GIVE is organized by Michael "Pinball" Clemons, and when he put out the call for people to come down and join him, you bet I volunteered! Sometimes, volunteering is just showing up.

School

School is the perfect place to get started volunteering as there are always things that teachers and students need help with. Sometimes this means getting involved in clubs, such as an eco-team where you can help take care of the recycling program. Or it could involve spending time with younger students in reading programs. I can think of dozens of ways to lend a hand at school. Since that's where we young people spend most of our time, it makes sense for us to get involved there!

Here's something really important to keep in mind when you're thinking about volunteering and making an impact: like all change, our actions add up. The most recent statistic I have to share with you is that WE calculated all of the volunteer hours that young people have logged through WE Schools since the program began, and the number is huge: **27 million hours**. Young people have also raised $79.8 million for more than 2,500 global and local causes. So your few hours here and there might not always seem like a lot, but when we all get involved, the result is huge, and it takes all of our hours and all of our giving to create it.

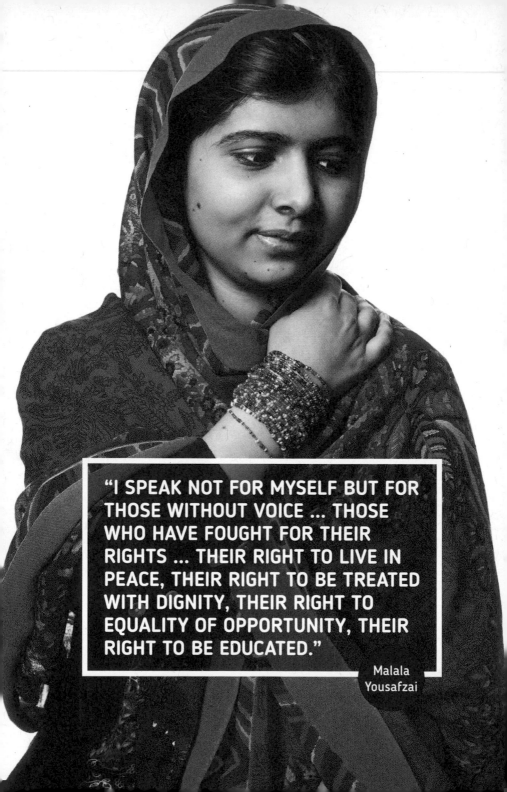

"I SPEAK NOT FOR MYSELF BUT FOR THOSE WITHOUT VOICE ... THOSE WHO HAVE FOUGHT FOR THEIR RIGHTS ... THEIR RIGHT TO LIVE IN PEACE, THEIR RIGHT TO BE TREATED WITH DIGNITY, THEIR RIGHT TO EQUALITY OF OPPORTUNITY, THEIR RIGHT TO BE EDUCATED."

Malala Yousafzai

MALALA YOUSAFZAI:
HUMANITARIAN, EDUCATION ACTIVIST, NOBEL PEACE PRIZE WINNER

Malala Yousafzai is a role model for me and for girls all over the world. In 2012, on her way home from school, Malala was attacked because she spoke and wrote about the importance of education for girls. She has not let that stop her, and she has inspired people of all ages all over the world to stand up for what they believe in, even if—sometimes especially if—it goes against the status quo.

On April 12, 2017, Malala received honorary Canadian citizenship from Prime Minister Justin Trudeau. Malala is only the sixth person ever to receive this honour (and the youngest). Afterward, Malala addressed Parliament in the House of Commons about the importance of girls' education and Canada's role in social justice in the world.

I was honoured to be invited by Malala and Prime Minister Trudeau to witness this incredible day. The highlight of the day, however, and perhaps of my journey so far and forever, happened when I was given the opportunity to sit down and interview Malala. I decided to leave our conversation as a straight Q&A, the way it happened.

Hannah: Malala, thank you so much for sitting down with me and for having this conversation. You've inspired me so much over the past five years: for me to know that you're never too young to make a difference. So now that you're an honorary Canadian, which is amazing, tell me some of the characteristics that Canada has that you think the world could follow.

Malala: Canada has shown great support toward women's rights, feminism, and refugees—it has been standing at the front. Also in bringing peace. I think that these are the key things we need to focus on right now. So I'm here to accept the honorary citizenship and meet amazing girls in Canada, amazing people here, and talk to them. It was just an incredible trip, and I'll always remember this as a really incredible moment and part of my life. The thing that I was pushing today was investment in education, and I think that if Canada leads in that, the world will follow in the footsteps of Canada, the world will learn from Canada. I think that investment in girls' education is the best way we can solve many of the issues we are facing.

❝ I think that **investment** in **girls' education** is the **best way we can solve** many of the **issues we are facing**. ❞

Hannah: We both started blogging when we were really young. Tell me about blogging in the early days.

Malala: So, I was 10 or 11 years old, and at that time, girls' education was banned by the terrorists, by the Taliban. I wanted to speak out because my right to go to school was taken away from me. And in that situation, when you know if you don't go to school, then just like other girls, you'll get married at an early age, that you'll never be able to achieve your dreams to become a doctor or a teacher—and that should be a basic human right of every woman, but you wouldn't have that right—that is why I started speaking out, and that was through blogging. It was for the BBC, and I did it under the pen name of Gul Makai, and I spoke out. I didn't know if it would have any impact or not, but I soon realized that a girl's voice is powerful, and it can bring change in a community. And then I continued my campaigning. I spoke to people, I spoke to the community, I spoke to the media as much as I could to make sure that we stood up for education and we stood up against the terrorism in our region.

My issue is girls' & women's right to education.

My gift is my voice.

Hannah: Something else both you and I have in common is that we both believe in the power of young people. We both know that our generation can, and already is, changing the world. Talk to me about the power of youth.

Malala: I think that people often say youth is the future and that their education and their well-being will affect each and every one of us. But I think that considering youth as the future is one side, but also accept them as the present. If youth do not have the right to education, if youth do not get the facilities of good health, and if they don't get equal opportunities, then it means that it is impacting each and every one of us. So I would say that youth—we often call them "future leaders"—are present leaders as well. They should step forward and believe in themselves.

Hannah: So many young girls around the world, including me, are inspired by you. Something that discourages people sometimes is that they don't have money to donate to a cause or issue they care about. How can people, particularly youth, make a difference that doesn't involve money?

Malala: I think that in order to go forward, you need to believe in yourself. You need to be your biggest supporter and your best friend. If you don't believe in yourself, you cannot go forward. I always considered myself as a mature person, right from the

The change is helping girls and women gain access to education.

beginning. And that was also because my father believed in me. He allowed me to talk, and he would listen to me carefully. I think that your parents and your community can play a big role in that— that they listen to you, that they give importance to your voice, and then you start realizing that yes, your voice really matters. Even if you are young, it doesn't matter.

Also, we have so many tools, like being on social media, having access to blogging, and just having the opportunity to meet friends and meet your community that really doesn't need much financial support. So those are really the ways in which you can engage with people, bring people together, and share your thoughts and views with them. Use social media for that. And I think your voice is the most important thing. If you have your voice, then nothing can stop you. If you believe in yourself, then nothing can stop you.

> " I think **your voice** is the **most important thing**. If you have **your voice**, then **nothing can stop** you. If you **believe in yourself**, then **nothing can stop you**. "

Malala Yousafzai

THE GIRL WHO STOOD UP FOR EDUCATION

As part of the WE Day Tour in 2013/2014, I shared Malala's story and the ways that she inspires me with more than 100,000 people in 10 stadiums across North America. I always opened with, "Another world changer was born in Pakistan; her name is Malala." To this day, it remains one of my greatest honours. It always will.

To fully understand who Malala is today, it's important to look at the events that shaped her life. Malala was born in 1997 and grew up in Mingora, a town in the Swat District of northwest Pakistan, with her parents and two younger brothers. Her father, Ziauddin, was the teacher and headmaster of the school that Malala attended. Malala loved going to school and had plans to become a doctor. She had a great life in a beautiful place. That is, until 2007 when the Taliban invaded Swat Valley and started to take away pieces of people's lives—music, television, equality, and education.

In 2009, Malala began to write a blog for BBC Urdu. Using a pen name, Gul Makai, she wrote her first blog post on January 3. Malala wrote about her life under the rule of the Taliban and about the fear she had about her school, her home, and her family being attacked.

"Malala has shown us that you are not too young to understand, to care, to be heard, and to DO something."
—Hannah Alper, Daughters for Life Gala speech

On January 14, 2009, Malala's school closed. But in February, it appeared that peace might happen in the area, and the girls' schools reopened. Peace didn't happen, however, and the fear and violence became worse.

When the Taliban banned all girls from going to school, Malala blogged about what was happening. She was featured in a documentary for the *New York Times*. She gave interviews and spoke out in public. From this time forward, she was known to the world—and also to the Taliban. She had given a name, face, and voice to her outspoken desire and right to go to school.

In 2011, Malala was awarded Pakistan's first National Youth Peace Prize and was nominated by Archbishop Desmond Tutu for the International Children's Peace Prize. In response to her rising popularity and national recognition, Taliban leaders voted to kill her.

On October 9, 2012, Malala was on a bus coming home from school. A masked gunman boarded the school bus looking for Malala. He threatened to kill everyone if she didn't stand up. Malala stood up. She was shot in the head.

Malala was flown to Birmingham, England, for care, and spent six months recovering in the hospital. When she was better, she did not hesitate to take action, and her voice was even louder—and now it was on a massive global scale.

"As a youth activist myself, Malala's influence has become a force and a role model for me, my peers, and for my generation. To us, you see, she is ours."
—Hannah Alper, Daughters for Life Gala speech

Malala is a powerful and strong activist for equality, education, and youth empowerment. She knows that education is the key to opportunity, and it is her goal that every child have the right to an education. There are 130 million youth not in school around the world. She says that if we don't act—if the world does not act—these young people will be a lost generation. Through her organization, the Malala Fund, she is raising money and awareness, and encouraging the world to act.

On her 16th birthday, Malala addressed the United Nations. Her words will stay with me forever: "I speak not for myself, but for those without voice." In 2014, at the age of 16, she won the Nobel Peace Prize, becoming the youngest person ever to receive this honour.

So you see why I am so inspired by her. Despite everything she has gone through, Malala has made it her mission to stand up for what she believes in, despite the personal risk. She started her activism at such a young age, and at only 19 years old, she is one of the most well-known activists in the world.

"Girls from all over the world now know that their voices matter, and when our voices are added together we are stronger."

—Hannah Alper, Daughters for Life Gala speech

I've had a special relationship with Malala since that first time I spoke on the WE Day stage. Backstage (in Toronto), I met Eason Jordan, who works closely with Malala at the Malala Fund. He congratulated me on my speech and the work I had done, and over the years we have kept in touch. The following year it was announced that Malala was going to be given honorary Canadian Citizenship in a ceremony in Ottawa. I was back on tour with WE Day for my second year, and I was in Vancouver the day the ceremony was taking place. Eason reached out to me and asked if I would like to meet with Malala back in Toronto the next day. I changed my flight so I could leave right after WE Day and meet her the next morning.

I was up early doing a live media interview for WE Day, which was interrupted with breaking news—a gunman had shot and killed a guard on Parliament Hill in Ottawa. There was very little information known right after the attack, and to ensure Malala's safety, Prime Minister Harper recommended that she leave. I received a phone call from Eason explaining that they had to leave, but asking if I was able to have a Facetime call with Malala. I found a quiet place (Nick Jonas's dressing room) and spoke to Malala for 20 minutes. I'll never forget it.

My phone rang and it was her father, Ziauddin. We spoke for a few minutes. He told me that he had watched the video of me speaking about Malala at WE Day. He told me he was proud of me, then he said, "I'm not going to be a wall between you and your sister, Malala." And there she was, on my phone. We talked about school and what we wanted to be when we grew up. We talked about travelling and what we like to do for fun. I did take the opportunity to ask her a couple of questions. At the time, she was still mostly being called "the girl who was shot," and I asked her how she wanted to be known. She said, "the girl who stood up for education." From that moment on, that's how I referred to her.

In May 2016, Malala was being honoured at a gala with the Courage and Inspiration Luminary Award by Daughters for Life, a foundation based in Toronto that supports education for girls in the Middle East by providing scholarships. Malala couldn't attend, but her parents were flying to Toronto to accept the award on her behalf. I was asked to address her parents when they accepted the award. It was such an honour standing before them and telling them how much Malala meant to me and my generation.

I have always been proud to be a Canadian, but April 12, 2017, will always be my proudest day. Prime Minister Justin Trudeau invited Malala to come back to Canada to accept her honorary Canadian citizenship. Eason reached out to me again, this time with an even more exciting opportunity than years earlier. He invited me to attend the ceremony and be in the House of Commons for Malala's official public address. A few days later, the official invitation came from Prime Minister Justin Trudeau and Malala.

It was an incredible day! We attended the official ceremony in the Library of Parliament, where Malala received her citizenship and was gifted with a Canadian flag from the Peace Tower. We were then escorted into the House of Commons for Malala's address. Hearing her speak for the first time in person was surreal.

She spoke with such passion, drive, and charm. I lost count of the standing ovations that happened throughout her speech. She included a message for us young Canadian girls:

"Young women of Canada, step forward and raise your voices. The next time I visit, I hope I see more of you filling these seats in Parliament."

At the end of the day, I was so honoured to have the opportunity to sit down and have a one-on-one conversation with Malala, which I shared a few pages ago. Just for fun, after our interview, we sat on the floor at a coffee table and I gave Malala the opportunity to show off one of her hidden talents: we played "The Cup Song."

"IT IS IN EVERYONE'S BEST INTEREST TO BE A PART OF THE SOLUTION."

Mitch
Kurylowicz

MITCH KURYLOWICZ:
FOUNDER OF PROJECT JENGA, MOTIVATIONAL SPEAKER, CHANGE-MAKER

When I think about young people who are creating tangible change, I always think of Mitch Kurylowicz. When he was 12 years old, he travelled to Kenya with ME to WE and attended the opening of Kisaruni, WE's first free all-girls secondary school. He asked a question that would change the course of his life and the lives of an entire community: "Is there a school for boys?" The answer? No.

Mitch was shocked. Where would the friends he had made playing soccer go to high school? He turned his shock into action. When he returned home to Ottawa, he formed Project Jenga (jenga means "to build" in Swahili). Its mission was to raise money for a boys' high school in Kenya so boys could have the opportunity to have a better future.

Six years later, Mitch had raised over one million dollars, and Ngulot All Boys Secondary School opened in January 2017 with 33 students, who had earned their spots through academic performance. (Ngulot means "strength" in Swahili.) The school is the first free all-boys' secondary school in Kenya. See what I'm talking about when I say Mitch is a young person making huge change?

My issues are education & opportunity.

I attended the official opening of Ngulot. It was exciting to be there for such a momentous event. There was phenomenal pride for the entire community knowing that there was a new opportunity for their youth to go to school. My family and I were so happy to celebrate with the community, WE, and Mitch's family.

Raising a million dollars isn't easy. How did Mitch get people to believe in him and in what he was doing?

"I remember being really shy and standing in front of my high school, shaking in my little T-shirt, my jeans, and my pair of shoes, and asking, 'Will anyone help me help these kids?' I didn't know what I was doing. I said, 'Look, these are my friends. These are people I've played soccer with. They're just like you. They're just like me. They're just like all of us. So will you help me?'"

Mitch raised $5,000 at his high school in just two weeks selling stickers that read "It's cool to be kind." He had received the stickers for free because a businessman saw a young student who wanted to make a real difference. The businessman listened to Mitch and offered what he had to help.

Mitch told me it was unbelievable how great the response was, seeing how much people cared about others halfway across the world in a country they'd never heard of, kids they've never met.

My gift is helping others to identify how they can help.

He'll never forget the moment when he realized how important education was to his friends in Kenya:

"I watched kids line up at schools made of cow dung, mud, and sticks. They waited and waited ... for a pencil. Hundreds and hundreds of kids lining up on this field, waiting for a pencil. [...] So while every one of my friends back home was looking to get the latest Xbox and latest soccer ball for themselves, my new friends in Kenya were looking for pencils and looking to go to school."

That image really stuck with Mitch and ignited his spark.

"It became a daunting task. I knew how much money and time it would take. I was a full-time student, still am [Mitch now attends the University of Toronto], and I wanted to raise this money. It was more the time than the money that was daunting. But I knew I was going to do it because I cared. I cared about my friends and I wanted to help them. I knew that school [Ngulot] would happen at some point in my life."

Something else I admire about Mitch is that he realizes you cannot do everything alone—community is essential when creating change. No one can raise a million dollars alone.

Mitch Kurylowicz

"I'm happy to be a small ripple in this bucket of empowerment. But, what I've done, and what the people who have helped me have done, is create this ripple, and it just keeps going."

Attending the school's opening was amazing for me; I could only imagine how it felt for Mitch. He said it was a highly emotional time for him when he met with the first students to attend Ngulot.

"The students in the classroom went around the room, saying their name, this is what I want to do, this is how old I am, this is what community I'm from. Afterwards, we sat in a circle and just talked. We talked through broken English, broken Swahili, a little bit of this and that. It was a real freeing, no judgment, no barriers, just talking. I told them they were the leaders in their communities already."

With all the success Project Jenga has achieved, Mitch said he has no plans to stop raising money. (Even though the costs to build the initial school have been paid for, money still needs to be raised to ensure that students can attend for free.)

"Why would I stop? Why would I quit doing something that makes me happy, that makes other people happy, that makes 33 kids go to school, that makes their communities happier because their kids are going to school? It's such a huge ripple effect that there would be no point for me to stop doing it."

The change is making more opportunities available to more people.

Mitch has plans to raise more money to build more new classrooms and a soccer field, and to provide school scholarships. Mitch has worked hard over the years and his project proved to be a success. I asked him to share some advice for people of all ages who want to make a difference.

"Ask questions, of course. And actually listen to people's answers. Don't just ask them because you're supposed to ask them. Find something you love to do, an honest love. You'll know .it's an honest love if you're selflessly committed to it. Then pursue it. Go for it. Whatever it is, whatever makes you happy, do it. Be ambitious and take risks. Be brave, but do it because you love it and it makes you happy."

" Find something **you love** to do, **an honest love**. You'll know it's an honest love if you're **selflessly committed** to it. Then **pursue it. Go for it. "**

STEP SOMEWHERE NO ONE HAS STEPPED BEFORE

Mitch's advice is worth repeating: do it because you love it. He has spent time every year in Kenya since he founded Project Jenga and has truly become part of the community. Now that I have spent time there myself, it feels like a second home. I went to Kenya for the first time in June 2016 and again in December that year.

My time in December was a particularly special trip to celebrate some huge milestones for WE and the community in the Maasai Mara in Kenya. The first was the graduation ceremony, class of 2016, for Kisaruni All Girls Secondary School. It was the first graduating class that included the girls from the second campus. Hundreds of people from the community celebrated with the girls and their families. That's what you learn very quickly in Kenya—it's all about the community. You knew that you were witnessing incredible change through the achievements and dreams of these girls.

The second milestone was the opening of Ngulot. That's right: the first free all-boys secondary school in Kisaruni—the school that Project Jenga funded. Mitch, of course, was there too, and so were his parents, aunt, grandmother, friends, and community members.

In addressing the crowd, one of the community elders said something I will never forget: "Now that we have both the girls' and the boys' high schools, our community is complete."

Secondary school is not free for students in Kenya. There are fees to pay to attend secondary school, so if your family cannot afford it, you don't go. Poverty is a barrier to many things, including clean water, health care, food, and education. It is education that will provide opportunities to lift people, families, and communities out of poverty. Education is the gateway to a good job and a future.

So this is why this school was so important to Mitch and to the community he has grown to love. Through the opening of the school, 33 boys now have the opportunity to go to school tuition-free, having earned their spots through academic performance. Attending high school was an opportunity they never would have had because their families simply could not afford the fees.

On the morning of the opening of Ngulot, we went to visit one of the students at his home. His name is Hazard, and here is a story he wrote about himself in third-person:

Hazard comes from Emori Joi community. He hails from a single parent (father only) family. The father burns charcoal as his only means to get money. Hazard has other two siblings. One of them is at Enelerai Secondary and has total fee arrears of Ksh30,000 [$392 CDN]. The other brother missed the whole of second term due to lack of school fees. Friends and well-wishers supported him through his third term.

The family land size is about 1.5 hectares with only one cow, with no sheep, goats, or chickens. Hazard sat for the national exams last year and did not proceed to high school due to lack of fees. He decided to repeat Grade 8 so that he could try his luck in getting a spot at the new boys' school in Kisaruni. The boy is good in academics and normally scores high in academics.

Hazard stands out because despite the challenges he has gone through, like having to be brought up by his grandmother after his mother's death while his father struggled to fend for them, he has always maintained his focus toward excellence in education. The father's income cannot even afford them a decent meal, leave alone an education. Hazard has gone through a myriad of challenges but managed to overcome and do well in his primary education.

Many of the boys in this first class at Ngulot are the first in their family to go to secondary school. Hazard was not the only one who repeated Grade 8 so that he would have the opportunity to apply to be one of those students. Three hundred and eighty-five boys applied for 33 spots.

When I went to Kenya for the first time, I laid bricks for what is now a classroom at Ngulot, and I was honoured to celebrate that day with Mitch, his family, and the community. My family and I hope to be there together again in 2021 to see Hazard and his classmates graduate. There is a Maasai saying, "If you step somewhere that no one has stepped before, you will make your own mark." These students are all stepping somewhere new and will each make his own mark. Just like Mitch did.

"DO IT AFRAID."

Maya
Penn

MAYA PENN:
ECO-DESIGNER, ENTREPRENEUR, ANIMATOR, CODER, AUTHOR

As CEO of Maya's Ideas—an eco-friendly clothing and accesso-ries company—Maya Penn is one busy 17-year-old. Her products are sold worldwide, and she donates 10% to 20% of the profits to local and global environmental organizations and other charities. Maya's book, YOU GOT THIS! Unleash Your Awesomeness, Find Your Path, and Change Your World, *was published in 2017. Oprah Winfrey chose Maya as one of her Supersoul 100 influencers, and Google partnered with her to speak to girls about coding. The TEDWomen Talk she gave in 2013 is ranked as one of the top 15 TEDWomen Talks of all time.*

There's more: Maya received a commendation from President Barack Obama and the United States Environmental Protection Agency for outstanding achievement in environmental steward-ship. Since the age of eight, Maya's been working hard to prove that you can use what you're good at to make a difference.

In February 2016, Maya and I spoke on the opening panel at the NFL Women's Summit, and we hung out for the weekend in Houston, Texas.

My issues are the environment & women's rights.

Because she has accomplished so much, my first question to Maya was what she's most proud of.

"The biggest thing would probably be when I was 13 and I did my TEDWomen Talk in San Francisco. It has almost two million views now. Even now, I get emails and comments from kids all over the world who were inspired to do something, and who want to follow their own passion."

Maya inspired me from the first time I watched her talk online. She has been inspiring others since she was only eight years old—when she became the CEO of Maya's Ideas.

"I started not only from a passion for fashion design, but wanting to do something that made a positive impact. I learned about the negative impacts that the fashion industry can have on the environment, so I knew when I started, that for that reason, I wanted all my items to be eco-friendly, which means they're made from materials that are not harmful to the environment, are organic, and are recycled."

Maya's designs are beautiful AND good for the planet. There are T-shirts, skirts, scarves, necklaces, earrings, purses, and more. There is almost nothing that Maya doesn't put her creative stamp on.

Maya took her change further when she launched her nonprofit organization called Maya's Ideas 4 the Planet. One of her campaigns was developing eco-friendly sanitary pads in developing communities. I asked her why that was important to her.

"In developing countries, a lot of the girls cannot go to school during their cycle because they don't have any sanitary pads to wear, which leads to them dropping out of school. It's crazy how that affects them in these countries. I've been having the pads shipped out to Somalia, Senegal, Cameroon, and Haiti. It's been really cool to see the impact it's been making." Thanks to Maya's efforts in these countries, girls are able to go to school and focus on their education.

One of Maya's interests is coding and computer science. She believes it's important for young people to develop these skills.

"You can create and build so many things with code, and it's really amazing the kind of world you open up with being able to use code. I think now more than ever, we're moving at such a technological pace. I think it's really important to tap into STEM [science, technology, engineering, and mathematics], which can be used in so many different ways to give back to the world. The sky's the limit because it's such a creative medium."

“ I think it's **really important** to tap into **STEM** [science, technology, engineering, and mathematics], which **can be used in so many different ways** to **give back to the world**. **”**

Maya Penn

My gift is my Creative Spirit.

Being involved in so many causes and running your own business isn't easy. Maya faced some obstacles along the way. I love what she had to say about that:

"You cannot avoid obstacles. If you think successful people have had it easy-breezy, and they made no mistakes and they hit no hurdles, then you are completely wrong. I've had obstacles being young and being a girl. People may not take you seriously when you say you're starting a business and you're an eight-year-old girl. And then people think it's cute, and it's just a game for me, but it's not."

She says what keeps her going are the emails and messages from girls, and seeing them being inspired by her to start their own businesses or give back to their communities. Maya told me she's learned a lot of lessons.

"One of the biggest lessons I've learned is that everyone has their own power, their own place, and their own way to positively impact the world, whatever way that is. When people see the types of issues happening all over the world, they think, 'I'm just a drop in the bucket. How can I possibly make a difference at all?' But every small action leads to a huge change whether you know it or not."

 Every small action leads to a **huge change** whether you know it or not. 🙶

Maya shared her thoughts on what young people can do to start making a difference.

"Find the cause that you're passionate about, do a lot of research on it, and find organizations or events that you can get involved with, whether that's volunteering or becoming a member of your youth division. Be educated on what it is that you're passionate about."

Maya also said that it's important to spread the word on social media. She believes we should discuss what we care about, share the events we're attending, and ask and encourage others to take action. I'm all for that.

I was curious to know what keeps Maya motivated doing what she does.

"What motivates me is knowing that what I've done with my business and nonprofit and activism is inspiring other youth to do whatever it is that they're passionate about and fight for the cause they believe in. I think it's really amazing that people of all ages are taking my message and implementing it into their lives and saying, 'Okay. Now this is what I want to do to give back.' It motivates me knowing that people have a head start because they've seen what I'm doing."

The change is bringing attention to issues I care about.

HANNAH'S REFLECTION

USING YOUR GIFT TO CREATE CHANGE

Maya is an awesome example of Issue + Gift = Change in action. She is passionate about many issues and she is using her many gifts to create change. Maya has worked tirelessly to use what she's good at to make a difference. She has used her gifts of animating, coding, fashion design, and entrepreneurism to raise awareness and funds for the issues she is passionate about. Maya and I both discovered our issues at a young age, and we've both identified many things we care about.

Sometimes you can become overwhelmed by really serious issues. You also might feel helpless. That's totally natural. But you cannot stay feeling upset, overwhelmed, and helpless. That's not good for anyone or anything. So you look at your gift—that thing that you're good at—and use it to help you make a difference.

A gift is all about using what you love to do or what you're good at to take action. Think about it. What is your gift? Well, it's likely you can use that to help others and take action on the cause you're passionate about. Everyone has something unique they can contribute to their home, school, neighbourhood, and beyond.

Here are 15 gifts and some ideas on how to use them to create change.

If you're athletic—volunteer to help coach a community team or organize a tournament. Players can pay to play and you can sell tickets to watch the game.

 If you're artistic—make posters to raise awareness for your issue or organize an art sale to raise money.

 If you're a musician—and you sing, play an instrument, or write songs, offer to perform at an event being held in your community.

 If you're good at keeping organized—help your school council or club with initiatives and campaigns and keep everything on track.

 If you're a good listener—be there for someone who needs to talk. When someone looks like they're having a bad day, ask them if they're okay and be there with an open ear.

 If you love writing—start a blog, write a guest post for a blog, or submit a story or letter to the editor for a newspaper or magazine you love. Share what you're passionate about.

 If you love to talk—offer to be the MC for an assembly at your school or event in your community. Get up on stage and share what matters to you!

 If you love photography or making videos—offer your skills to a group or an organization that could use visual support for their campaign. Offer to be the onsite photographer or videographer for an event.

Maya Penn

#9 If you love to bake or cook—host or contribute to a bake sale as a great, tangible way to raise funds and awareness for a cause you care about. Make meals or snacks to hand out to people who are homeless in your community.

 #10 If you love social media—use your accounts to share what you care about. Sharing what you're working on and sharing what the organizations you support are doing goes a long way toward raising awareness and mobilizing support.

 #11 If you love kids—offer to babysit and give a busy family a helping hand. Volunteer at a camp, after-school program, or event for kids.

 #12 If you're great at math or reading—offer to help students who need extra support with their homework or projects.

#13 If you're great at science and technology—apply those skills to seek solutions to problems. Some of the world's biggest challenges are overcome by STEM.

 #14 If you love gardening and being outside—volunteer to plant and care for gardens in your community or help out a neighbour who is elderly or ill.

 **#15** If you've got spare time—check out the volunteer opportunities in your communities. Time is also a gift you can give.

I realize it can be really nerve-wracking to get started making change. There might be some skeptical thoughts going through your head, such as "What if it doesn't work? What if nobody cares?" We're all prone to feeling vulnerable. But when you're thinking those thoughts, remember what Maya says: "Do it afraid."

When Maya said this to me, I remembered some advice I had been once given. It was one of my very first WE Days and I was honoured to co-host a special breakfast for educators. My co-host in every city was Martin Luther King III, who is Martin Luther King Jr.'s eldest son. I asked him if he ever gets nervous and he told me:

"Those nerves that you're feeling, those butterflies, it just means that you have lots of adrenaline. You're excited. If you're not at least a little bit nervous, it might mean that you shouldn't be doing what you're doing."

Now, I anticipate those nerves. I actually look forward to them. Those nerves make me excited to go out on stage and do it. It's okay to be afraid, especially when you believe in what you're doing. Do it afraid. EVERY TIME.

"YOU DON'T HAVE TO CHANGE THE WORLD IN A DAY, BUT YOU CAN CHANGE SOMEBODY'S WORLD IN A DAY."

Corinne Hindes

CORINNE HINDES:
HOMELESSNESS ACTIVIST, CO-FOUNDER OF WARM WINTERS

Corinne Hindes and her best friend, Katrine Kirsebom, are the co-founders of Warm Winters, an organization that collects warm clothes, socks, and personal care products and distributes them to homeless shelters. Corinne and Katrine inspire me because they prove that creating change isn't always about donating money.

The best friends started Warm Winters when they were 11 years old. One day in 2011, Corinne saw a man who was homeless on the street near her house. It was a really cold day and he was wearing only jeans and a T-shirt. Corinne wanted to help him. Fast-forward to ski practice. Corinne and Katrine noticed a huge pile of hats, coats, gloves, and scarves in the lost and found. They asked the resort if they could give the clothing to people experiencing homelessness in their community. The resort said yes, and that's how Warm Winters began.

Today, hundreds of Warm Winters' youth volunteers collect clothing from 36 ski resorts. They have delivered 31,000 items of warm clothing to 33,000 people in need. Talk about a ripple effect and the impact that people can make!

Corinne told me that the biggest obstacle was getting people to believe them when they called the ski resorts to ask for clothing.

"We would call and say, 'Hey, we want to take your lost and found items and donate them to the homeless.' They did not believe us because we were children. We would have to call a resort five times to get them to listen to what we had to say. People don't believe kids can make a difference, but some of the best ideas come from the youth in our communities. They see the pain of others and immediately think 'How can I help?'"

It's so true. Corinne said everything changed when they received an award from the Jefferson Awards Foundation in recognition of their efforts. The Jefferson Awards pays close attention to youth who are making a difference and helps to amplify their voice and mentor them. Co-founder Sam Beard helped Corinne and Katrine create an action plan to expand.

My issue is homelessness.

" People don't believe kids can make a difference, but **some of the best ideas** come from the youth in our communities. They see the pain of others and immediately think **'How can I help?' "**

Having benefited from being mentored themselves, Corinne and Katrine also inspire youth to join their efforts. Corinne told me a great story about what happened after they gave a presentation at a high school in Indiana. The students reached out to them on social media to tell them about the actions they were taking on homelessness in their community.

"They'd say, 'I started my own program with my school. I've been donating a lot of my stuff.' It's amazing to hear these stories because it really is like a water drop effect—you get one ripple, and that's us, and we are the drop, and suddenly, all these teens are doing their own projects and creating this big ripple in the water full of change."

When I heard this, I thought, "YES! I AGREE!" Little things DO add up to make a big difference. That's a model I live by. It's a huge myth that only big actions make a difference, but obviously, that's wrong.

One thing I needed to ask Corinne about was the stigma around homelessness and how we can change the way people react to those who are homeless. Corinne told me:

"People walk by homeless people in the streets every day and their reaction isn't 'This person needs help. Maybe I can do something.' Their reaction is usually to grab their child's hands, their

My gift is empathy.

purse, and look away. People need to realize these are people. That homeless man you walk by every Tuesday lost his job. Maybe he lost touch with his family or needs help getting onto his feet."

For Corinne, helping can mean little things, such as buying a person a sandwich, inviting them to sit down and have a meal with you, talking with them, or simply not looking away.

"All you have to do is look them in the eye and smile. A lot of people think, 'No, that's going to encourage them to hurt you.' And I say, 'They're not going to hurt you. They're people. All they want is for someone to actually see them and recognize their pain.' Nobody does that. Nobody looks at them. Everyone looks away and acts like they're not there because they wish they weren't."

Everyone deserves to be looked at as a person, as someone with humanity. Everybody deserves a second chance because, simply, why not?

Corinne said it's been amazing to watch Warm Winters grow and see how much she and Katrine have helped people.

"One of the most incredible stories I have is about that first homeless man we saw, Billy. He became a friend of ours. It's been amazing watching him grow from having nothing. Now he has a job, an apartment, and a car. He even got a dog. He's grown so much over the years and he's watched us grow into the young women we are, so it's been pretty amazing."

Corinne told me that working with her best friend, Katrine, has been incredible.

"We're passionate about helping others, and we have this bond. I always have someone to turn to. For example, if I have an idea, or I'm struggling, or I'm thinking about giving up, I always have Katrine to turn to and say, 'Hey, I don't know what to do.' We motivate each other. She is my rock and I am hers."

I know exactly what she means. When I started my blog, no one else was doing that at my school or in my community. When I found WE, I saw there were so many young, passionate people taking action on all different kinds of issues. I got what they were doing and they got me. We supported each other.

Corinne shared some great advice about how to start making change.

"One step a day is all you need to change the world, because if you take one step on Monday, and then another on Tuesday, and then another on Wednesday, all of a sudden, you're all the way over here, and it's only Friday. Imagine what you can do in an entire year. No action is too small because it all has to do with your end goal, which is creating change and making a difference."

The change is helping people get their lives started again.

IT'S NOT ALWAYS ABOUT MONEY

One of the biggest myths about making a difference is that it takes money to change the world. I bet when you think about creating change, you think about donating money to an organization or fundraising for a cause. That's fair. It's true for most people. Sometimes that feels like the type of change we hear about the most and often, and it makes it hard for people to be confident they can change the world.

But just like the story of Warm Winters showed us, sometimes what people need isn't money. Instead of giving money to people experiencing homelessness, Corinne gives different resources. Through Warm Winters, she gives clothes from the lost and found of ski resorts, charities, and corporations. Another way she gives is through conversation. She sits down with people and wants to know who they are and what their story is. She treats people who are homeless like ... well, people. Because they are. Doing this shows that someone cares and will have an open ear, mind, and heart. It could make a person's day just knowing that someone took the time to get to know them. After that, they could realize they have a second chance and get back up on their feet.

I'm 14 years old. I don't have a job and I don't have a whole lot of money that I can just set aside to donate. Let's be real. Most kids are in the same situation. But it's not just kids. Not everyone has the kind of money they would like to give to support issues that matter to them. At the risk of repeating myself, I'm going to say it again: making a difference is not always about money. There are many other ways you can make an impact without money. In fact, maybe there are so many ways you can make a difference that donating money is soon going to be seen as "the other way."

Here are 10 ways that do not involve giving or asking for cash:

#1 **Give compliments and/or high-fives.** Or both! Yeah, both. That's better. Believe it or not, giving a compliment to someone can brighten their day and make them smile, causing other people to smile, which causes that ripple effect. How cool is that? If someone is having a bad day, something as simple as a high-five, a compliment, or holding the door for them could change their day. While that may not change *the* world, it changes *their* world, and sometimes, that's enough.

#2 **Write a thank you note to a really cool person in your life.** It could be to a parent, guardian, educator, or someone who is just awesome and makes your day or life better. Tell them that. Knowing you've made a difference for someone is one of the best feelings there is. Let them feel that. (I included a thank you note I wrote on page 137. Maybe it'll give you some ideas for what you might write.)

High-five!

Shovel somebody's driveway or mow someone's lawn.
This makes a huge impact, especially if you're shovelling the driveway for an elderly or sick neighbour. Doing this might mean they get to go to the grocery store or make it to a doctor's appointment. Bam! You just changed the world.

Donate your hair to people going through cancer treatments. When people are going through chemotherapy, their hair often falls out. Environmental types, listen up—your hair is a renewable resource. If you cut your hair and donate it, you can change someone's life.

Help a friend with homework or a project they're working on. I appreciate it so much when my classmates help me with math that I missed while I was absent.

Donate your clothes, toys, or household items to a shelter or an organization that helps those in need in your community. I bet lots of you have clothes you hardly ever wear anymore and toys you've outgrown by now. If they are still in good condition, you can pass them on to someone who will really enjoy them (which is way more eco-friendly than just throwing them out).

Got some spare time? Get out there and do something with it. Participate in a neighbourhood cleanup, sort at a food bank, volunteer at a reading program, or plan a visit to a retirement centre.

Donate your voice. Take out your phone and tweet, retweet, post, and share information about issues and organizations you support. Help them get the word out about the important work they do.

That gift that you have? Use it. Are you great at art or graphic design? Are you an athlete and can help coach a local sports team? Offer your talent to an organization or a group in your community that might be under-resourced.

Write a letter. Have you had a really great experience at a local business? Write a letter to the owner to tell them they have some awesome people working with them.

And hey, if you have money to give, why not do the above things, too? Yeah, both!

Now I've come full circle and back to Corinne and her mantra, because it's worth repeating:

"You don't have to change the world in a day, but you can change somebody's world in a day."

Corinne Hindes

Hannah Alper ✓
@ThatHannahAlper

Follow

#2, done! I have high fived 10 people! High fives are a great way to show kindness and encouragement! #my24hrs

Retweets **4**   Likes **22**   ● ● ● ● 🔥 ● ● ● ●

2:47 PM - 29 Feb 2016

💬   ↻ 4   ♡ 22   ✉

Hannah Alper ✓
@ThatHannahAlper

Follow

Dropped off 3 tonnes of non-perishable food, on behalf of my school! It's the holidays, give back how you can.

Retweets **15**   Likes **59**   ● ● ● ● ● ● ● ● ●

5:56 PM - 18 Dec 2015

Dear Educators,

I use the term "educators" because I want to say something to everyone who works in our schools to make them safe, inclusive, and welcoming.

You probably don't hear these two words enough and you should hear them more often. So, on behalf of all the students you have inspired, encouraged, and supported, **THANK YOU**. Thank you for what you do inside and outside your regularly scheduled class time. Thank you for the extra help at lunch and after school, for making learning fun and meaningful, for supervising our clubs and teams, for making our classrooms and schools safe places, and for so, so much more.

A VERY special thank you to those of you who support those students like me. I know that it creates more work for you when we miss a class or a day or even a week to pursue our passion, whether that is sports, arts, or activism. I am so, so grateful for all you do to make sure I succeed both in and out of the classroom.

When school is a place where we can learn and discover who we are and who we can be, amazing things happen. When we learn about the world, we begin to understand our place in it. I hope we inspire you as much as you inspire us.

Thank you, and thank you again and again.
Hannah Alper and the students you've inspired

"LOVE IS THE WHY YOU SHOULD DO ANYTHING."

Brad Montague

BRAD MONTAGUE:
CREATOR OF KID PRESIDENT, WRITER, DIRECTOR

Brad Montague is the award-winning writer and creative director behind Kid President. Like me, you're probably one of the tens of millions of people who've watched the viral videos starring Brad's brother-in-law, Robby Novak, a.k.a. Kid President. They're funny, wise, and bursting with positivity. Brad and Robby make a great team—they're family.

I met Brad and Robby backstage at WE Day Seattle and we hung out in the Green Room. In person, just like in their videos and on social media, they draw you in with good vibes. Kid President was one of the first social media personalities to really stress how important it is to be kind to others and share the belief that "kids have voices worth listening to," so naturally, I'm a fan. Fun fact: I got a shout-out in Kid President's "Awesome Girls Rap" video alongside world-changing women of the past and present, like Maya Angelou and Malala Yousafzai.

I sat down with Brad in Toronto after we participated on a TIFF Kids panel on young people changing the world. And he's doing that—one video at a time.

My issue is Spreading positivity.

Brad never set out to change the world with his Kid President videos. In 2012, he and Robby wanted to create some fun videos for family and friends to make them laugh and think. Brad believed that kids had voices worth listening to.

"I wanted to make sure we were exploring universal truth using a child's voice, like through the lens of a child, because there's something really wonderful about seeing the world in a childlike way—not a childish way. A childish way is closed off and selfish and just wants. But a childlike way is open, and full of wonder and awe and innocence and possibility."

Brad told me he thought it would be really powerful to put out an image of a young boy who cared about things.

"My son was about to be born, and I was watching TV and I didn't see any young boys who cared about things. Anytime you saw them, they were just like, 'Oh, I don't care, I'm going to play a video game, whatever.' And I thought, 'a young boy who cares about stuff,' that could be something."

Brad began really focusing on what they were saying in the videos and what the messages meant. He tackled some important topics, such as bullying.

"We would take something very heavy like bullying and think, 'How can we do this where it doesn't feel like a sermon, and it doesn't feel like a classroom lesson—where it feels like a friend is talking to you in a silly way?' Friends can be jokey to each other and they laugh, but [then you] get to the heart of it. So [the subject] would always start with exploring it in a fun, light way so that we could get to the heavy stuff."

Kid President's videos spread messages of hope and joy. I asked Brad why he focused on those two things.

"My thought was we could create an oasis online where everything we put out is going to be contagious in the best way. For example, we asked people to send in videos of them laughing so we could make this super-cut video of just a bunch of people laughing. It would be this contagious video of putting more laughter in the world."

The laughing video is hilarious, and it makes you feel good. Brad told me they would post about things they wanted to see more of in the world—like laughing, dancing, being kind to others—with the idea that the more videos they made, the more those kinds of things would happen in real life.

My gifts are writing & filmmaking.

"We did this project where we wanted people to love their neighbours who are homeless, and people did it. On every single continent in the world, people who probably don't understand what is being said on the video somehow caught on to the idea."

Brad has an interesting take on his videos and creative work:

"I feel like my work is not mine; it's the world's. It's for everybody. And when everybody shows up in their unique way, they're adding to the symphony of humanity. You're adding your note that is desperately needed. I legitimately need every person to add their note to this thing we're trying to do."

I really love what he said because he's getting at something that plays a huge role in my understanding of social good, and that's community. We're all good at different things, so we need to bring them together. Like Brad and Robby, we need to be a team. Call it a symphony, a club, or a squad—it's about doing it together. Teamwork makes the dream work. That's what I say.

It all adds up. That's exactly what I've been getting at, and like Brad says, if we all *show up*, we can do this.

> **66** When **everybody shows up** in **their unique way**, they're **adding** to the **symphony of humanity**. You're **adding your note** that is desperately needed. **99**

I think one of the reasons people are so inspired by Brad and Robby is their message about kindness. It's a topic I'm passionate about, too. Kid President is known for saying "Treat everybody like it's their birthday!" I asked Brad, "Why that message?"

"Well, we're all in this together. We're all here. Robby and I do [these videos] as a family. We're on a mission together. And I think in the same way, human beings are on a mission together. It would be pretty great if humankind was full of kind humans."

Brad believes young people have the ability to unlock goodness wherever they go. When you watch Kid President's videos, you can see adults opening up to Robby, whether it's a politician (he hung out with President Obama in the Oval Office) or a musician (yes, he really did kiss Beyoncé).

Do you know why adults open up? I think it's because Robby's having fun and he's not afraid to show it. The other thing I've picked up on from Brad and Robby is that they are really passionate about the issues they tackle and the way they tackle them. I don't know about you, but every Kid President video I watch makes me feel good and hopeful. You know what that makes me want to do? Pass it on.

The change is making the world a better, more positive place.

Brad Montague

SPACE JAM AND STAR POWER

In Kid President's most viral video, "A Pep Talk from Kid President to You," he asks, "What will be your *Space Jam*?" If you haven't seen the video, you might be thinking, what is he talking about? What does that even mean? *Space Jam* is one of Robby's favourite movies—it stars basketball legend Michael Jordan, who saves the planet from an alien invasion. So what Robby figures is this: if Michael Jordan had quit playing basketball after he didn't make the team in high school, he never would have made *Space Jam*. "And I love *Space Jam*," he says. For Robby, *Space Jam* is one of those things that makes the world awesome. So the question becomes "What will you create that will make the world awesome?" His answer: "Nothing, if you keep sitting there!"

This question motivated the 40+ million people who have watched the video (so far), and Robby's brother-in-law, Brad, said he made the pep talk video because he needed a pep talk. When the video launched and began receiving a lot of traction, Brad was really motivated by that *Space Jam* line. But then he had a thought that scared him a bit: "What if that video was my *Space Jam*?" He wondered, if that was his *Space Jam*, whether that meant he wasn't going to do anything else that would make the world awesome.

OPEN your EYES!
YOUR LIFE is ENCHANTED.
WHATEVER you
DO PLEASE
DON'T TAKE
IT FOR
GRANTED!

However, Brad realized that your *Space Jam*—what you do to make the world awesome—is not one thing: "It is your entire life, and that adds up. And sometimes those chapters include failure, sometimes those chapters include regrets or sadness, but it all adds up to something really beautiful; if you are working to live a life with imagination and intention, it's going to add up to a masterpiece. Your life will be your *Space Jam*." Mic drop.

Robby said something that I really love: "You were made to be awesome." When you live with that intention, incredible things will happen, I promise. Not only will you feel awesome, but the world will be more awesome. He's not just referring just to you, though, but to everyone. Everyone was made to be awesome. So when we treat everyone like they're awesome, the world is better ... and, well, *awesome*.

Robby also puts this idea another way when he says in his video, "Treat everyone like it's their birthday." When it's someone's birthday, we all go out of our way to make the day special. We give them cards that tell them how special they are and serve cake covered in icing and candles, and we sing. Of course, you don't have to do those exact things every day to "treat everyone like it's their birthday"; it's about treating them like they're special—because they are. It's about honouring special things about people (and yourself) every day.

Anyone who knows me knows that one of my favourite shows of all time is *Pretty Little Liars*. I am proud to say I have watched all seven seasons. The TV series is based on the book series by the same name, and I've read all of them, too. If you don't know what it's about, it's basically a show where five teenagers are getting stalked and bullied, and they're on a mission to find the culprit known only as "A." Now, you might be thinking, "Hannah, I think you're getting off track. What does *that* have to do with being awesome and making the world a better place?"

Let me explain. In the first book, one of the girls, Spencer, described something she did with her family every night: Star Power. While she was convinced that her parents had gotten the idea from a company team-building retreat, it was something she looked forward to every day. At the dinner table, everyone shared their biggest achievement of the day, their Star Power.

When I read this, I loved the idea and decided to add Star Power to my family's dinner conversation. From that night on, my mom, dad, and I each share something we're proud of that happened in our day. Sometimes they are big achievements (like when I was asked to write this book) and sometimes they're smaller ones (like when I felt I did really well on a math test or helped a friend out with something). No achievement is too big or small for this activity. It's a great way to share daily awesome things that are going on in your life. And on those days that you don't feel are special or stand out, it makes you dig a little deeper to find the awesome, feel-good moments.

I can tie this whole thing back to Robby to say that those Star Power moments are bursts of *Space Jam*s and birthdays. By taking the time to call those things out and celebrate them, we all feel like at the end of the day we had at least one moment of awesome. My family decided to take Star Power a step further when we created a tradition called "Our Year in a Jar."

My mom bought some large glass jars and we each decorated a jar and added our name to it. The jars sit on top of a cabinet in our living room with a pen and stack of small papers in a bowl next to them. Every time something really cool, funny, or interesting happens, we leave a note with the date on it and put it in the jar of the person that we were with or that it happened to. Then on New Year's Eve, while we are sitting on the couch watching the live broadcast from Times Square in New York, we open the jars and take turns reading our notes. It's a great way to reminisce about all the special, funny, or just all-around awesome things that happened to each of us throughout the year. Similar to Star Power, it doesn't have to be something really big; it can just be a kind memory that will make you feel good.

We should all celebrate the awesome things that happen in our daily lives, and celebrate each other's accomplishments, as well. This doesn't even need to be something we do every day, but it's something we can do to develop a habit of recognizing ourselves and others for something that went really well.

"EVERY day
MAY NOT
be good ...
but THeRe'S
SoMeTHing
good iN
EVERY day."

—Alice MoRse EaRle

"NEVER GIVE UP."

Muzoon
Almellehan

MUZOON ALMELLEHAN:
EDUCATION ADVOCATE, UNICEF GOODWILL AMBASSADOR

Eighteen-year-old Muzoon Almellehan is on a mission: she wants to ensure that children in refugee camps have access to education. Muzoon herself is a refugee from Syria. In 2013, because of the civil war in her country, Muzoon and her family fled to Jordan, a neighbouring country in the Middle East. They lived in Zaatari, one of the largest refugee camps in the world; according to the UNHCR, the UN Refugee Agency, 80,000 people live in Zaatari, half of them children. Muzoon and her family then moved to Azraq, another refugee camp. The UNHCR estimates that there are more than 53,000 refugees in Azraq, and like in Zaatari, half of them are children. Each time they moved, Muzoon worried about her education. Would it be possible to go to school in a refugee camp?

It's no surprise Muzoon was worried. The UNHCR estimates 900,000 school-age Syrian refugees do not attend classes. Muzoon did go to class thanks to the tented schools run by UNICEF and Save the Children. But not all of her peers did. Muzoon decided to do something about it.

Muzoon and I were both featured in the *FASHION Magazine* article "The New First Ladies in Politics: The Politicians and Social Activists Who Are Changing the World." Muzoon and I connected on Instagram and set up time to talk "in person" via Skype from her home in the United Kingdom.

Muzoon is putting a spotlight on the importance of education for refugee children. One of my first questions to her was, "What was your life like in Syria?"

"Before the war, it was normal life and everything was safe. We had no problems. Everything was perfect, actually. All of us were preparing for our futures and also going to school, doing our daily activities, and we didn't worry about anything because there was no war and conflict. Syria is a beautiful country and also rich in history."

The war began in 2011, but it was in 2013 that Muzoon's family, concerned for their safety, decided they needed to leave.

"It was difficult for us, and my family didn't actually want to leave Syria because everything was there for me: my country,

My issue is ensuring refugee children have access to education.

which I was born in, and also my friends, my school, and especially my education. I thought if I left Syria, then maybe I would not find education in the camps."

Muzoon was able to continue her education; however, she witnessed something that shocked her.

"I was saddened and shocked when I saw many girls and boys who thought education was not important, not a priority like early marriage or child labour."

Muzoon knew she needed to make people understand the importance of education—that even in the refugee camps, it had to be a priority. This was especially true for girls, as she saw young girls being married off by their parents—they hoped having a husband would protect their daughters and secure their futures. Muzoon thought education was the way to a brighter future.

"I started a campaign to encourage the children. I advised them about the importance of education and the value of educated people. I told them we can do anything with education. First, we need to gain our right to education, then we could do anything we want, because if we are not educated, we will be faced with many challenges."

Muzoon's campaign started with individual conversations with children, followed by speaking with parents, and then to whole schools. UNICEF and Save the Children noticed her actions and she became an unofficial ambassador for the organizations.

Syria's Civil War has affected the lives of millions of people:

- 13.5 million Syrians need humanitarian aid.
- More than 5 million Syrians have fled their country.
- Almost half of these refugees are under 18 years old.
- 6.3 million people are displaced within Syria.
- 470,000 Syrians are estimated dead or missing.

Muzoon Almellehan

My gift is my education.

It wasn't easy. Muzoon faced resistance from some parents and children.

"The people who didn't listen to me, they gave me strong motivation to do *more* because that means there are still people who don't believe in education. I need to speak with them and let them know the value of education and the importance of educating children."

Muzoon and Malala Yousafzai met in February 2014 when Malala visited the Zaatari refugee camp. They stayed in contact by email and Skype and became friends. When Malala accepted her Nobel Peace Prize in December 2014, Muzoon was Malala's guest. Their friendship is a special one.

In 2016, Muzoon and her family moved to Newcastle, England. Malala lives in Birmingham, England. Together they have spoken with world leaders, asking them to spend money on educating refugee children. As of September 2016, Canada has contributed $143 million to refugee education.

The night before I met Malala, Muzoon expressed her gratitude to Canada in a message to me on Instagram. (See it on the right!)

I asked Muzoon for advice on what we can do to help her cause.

"Think deeply about the issues of refugees and especially the children. Think about them as humans, not as refugees, because most people think about refugees' basic needs like food and shelter, but they don't think about their future, and they don't think to give them skills like education."

Muzoon told me she would like to return to Syria to help rebuild her country.

"I would like to go back as a positive and strong person. I would like to go back with a strong, educated generation. From now on, I'm preparing myself to be an educated person and a person who really wants to do something for my country."

April 11, 2017 at 4:45 PM

GOOD LUCK tomorrow, I'm sure you'll spend an amazing time with the beautiful soul Malala, and the amazing prime minster of Canada. Sending you all my best and send my regards and thanks to Malala and to the PM who are standing with people everywhere and I hope to meet him someday in person and thank him and the Canadian people. Lots of love🖤🖤

April 12, 2017 at 8:43 AM

YOU ARE AMAZING!!!

The change is education for every boy and girl.

Muzoon Almellehan

EDUCATION IS POWER

When I launched my blog and started taking action, I was looking at the issues I could see right in front of me. I had a deep connection to the environment because it was all around me. I could see my actions making a difference. At 10 years old, you don't really look beyond what is right in front of you. And that's okay.

When I went to WE Day the first time, I started to learn about global issues, and the whole world became what was right in front of me. I had never considered myself lucky that I could turn on the tap and get a glass of water. I had never considered myself lucky because I got to go to school every day.

Let's look at some numbers:

32 million primary-aged girls around the world are not in school.

98 million more girls are missing out on secondary education.

In total, more than **130 million** girls are out of school today.

103 million youth worldwide lack basic literacy skills; more than **60%** of them are female.

Statistics from the Malala Fund.

Those are overwhelming numbers. (For some perspective, the population of Canada is 36 million in 2017.) For a young girl living in the suburbs in Canada, this was all a lot to take in.

momentus

But I have never been the kind of person who looks the other way, whether that is looking at issues close to home, such as homelessness or bullying, or global issues, such as access to clean water or education.

Now let's take a look at why so many girls aren't in school and what that means.

There are many reasons, and none of them are good. Sometimes it's because of poverty—school is not free in many countries, and often families simply cannot afford the fees to send children (girls and boys) to school. Sometimes it's because girls are needed to help at home by caring for younger siblings or helping out with chores, such as getting water. (Getting clean water, as I have learned and seen for myself, can literally take all day.) Sometimes girls don't go to school because they are married at a young age and are starting and caring for families of their own. Sometimes there is violence in the area and it is not safe to go to school. Sometimes there just aren't enough schools to serve the potential students in a community. Sometimes poor sanitation, health problems, and lack of access to health care are what makes going to school impossible.

"Girls must get education. Education is power. Education is the future. Education makes us who we want to be."

—Muzoon Almellehan at the Supporting Syria and the Region conference in London, U.K., February 4, 2016

Here are more stats I found while researching:

An estimated 50% of out-of-school children of primary-school age live in conflict-affected areas.

Girls living in conflict-affected countries are 90% more likely to be out of secondary school than those living in peaceful areas.

Every year, 15 million girls under the age of 18 become wives—an average of 40,000 every day. Over 60% of child brides in developing countries have no formal education.

A child born to a literate mother is 50% more likely to survive past the age of five. Over the past four decades, the global increase in women's education has prevented more than 4 million child deaths.

So what's being done to try to help these children? A lot, actually. In September 2015, 193 world leaders met to discuss ways to transform our world. They agreed to 17 Global Goals for Sustainable Development. (Goal number 4 is to achieve universal primary education.) If these goals are achieved, it would mean the end of extreme poverty, inequality, and climate change by 2030. This could happen in our lifetime. This is not something that any generation before us has been able to say.

Education is the key that will allow many other Sustainable Development Goals to be achieved. When people are able to get quality education, they can break from the cycle of poverty.

Education also empowers people everywhere to live more healthy and sustainable lives. Education is crucial to fostering tolerance between people and contributes to more peaceful societies.

When I went to Kenya, I saw all of these things for myself. That last point about peaceful societies, I learned, is particularly true. One of the most important outcomes of the Kisaruni All Girls Secondary School is the peace it has brought to the area. Carol, the headmaster of Kisaruni, explains on page 161 where the name itself comes from.

My favourite days in Kenya were the ones I got to spend at Kisaruni All Girls Secondary School. When I was there in June 2016, I spent a day with the Grade 10 class at the Milimani Campus both in and out of their classroom. We talked about our lives, our futures, our favourite school subjects, hobbies, and music.

I was lucky enough to be back in Kenya in December to attend the graduation celebrations for Kisaruni. One of the graduates was my friend Purity. I met Purity several years ago when she came to speak at WE Day along with Carol, the headmaster of Kisaruni. When I was in Kenya in June, Purity spent the day with me and gave me a tour of the Oleleshwa campus. We had an instant connection. Purity was the leader of the Journalism Club

Muzoon Almellehan

and wants to be a news reporter. I was unaware that she was in the graduating class, and when I saw her walk out in her cap and gown, I was so excited to see her! She didn't know I was going to be there, either, and it made the day extra special for us both.

It was a particularly special graduation because it was the first graduating class from the second campus at Oleleshwa. This was my all-time favourite day in Kenya for so many reasons. It was truly a celebration, and a few hundred community members joined the families of the graduates to mark these milestone moments for everyone.

It is important to remember that most of these girls are the first girls in their families to graduate from high school. Many of them will go to university and return as teachers at WE schools or doctors at Baraka. They WILL be great leaders and role models in their community and beyond. They already are. If it weren't for Kisaruni, none of them would imagine these goals were within their reach.

Kisaruni: The Centre for Peace

By Carol, Headmaster, Kisaruni All Girls Secondary School

Kisaruni Milimani campus is located at the border between the Kipsigis and Maasai communities, and the current location of the school was their battleground. The Maasai believed that all cattle belonged to them, and historically, they raided the Kipsigis homesteads and took their cows. This resulted in the two communities always fighting over cattle.

For the first time in their history, elders from both communities came to a common place at the ground-breaking for the high school. This common place was known for war and not for peace. On arrival, the Kipsigis elders sat at one side, far from the Maasai elders. They had to make a choice between a bright future for their children and continued war. They chose the education of their children.

The most challenging aspect was when the elders were asked which values they wanted instilled in their children. They both spoke about a school that respects and upholds the cultural values that they teach their children at home and a school where there will be peace and where each learner feels welcome and feels like she is at home.

The elders walked home calmly and happily, somehow with the assurance that change had come. A new dawn had been achieved. The battleground had been lost to the future of their children.

The school is therefore known as the centre for peace. Learners in the school live as sisters despite coming from the two previously warring communities.

"LEAD WITH LOVE."

Amanda Jetté Knox

AMANDA, ZOE, & ALEXIS KNOX:

LGBTQ+ RIGHTS ACTIVISTS

Amanda, Zoe, and Alexis Knox are courageous and compassionate women who love and support each other unconditionally. They have emerged as strong voices and advocates for LGBTQ+ rights. Amanda is a wife, mom, and award-winning blogger. Her blog, Maven of Mayhem, is open, honest, and raw, and that's where I first came to know her and her family.

Let me tell you what Amanda has been writing about lately. Her daughter, Alexis, came out as a transgender girl in 2014. It was an amazing story of bravery, love, and acceptance. In a March 2016 blog post, Amanda revealed another life-transforming happening in her family, sharing that her husband of 19 years had come out to her as a transgender woman, Zoe. Zoe was inspired by Alexis's courage and the acceptance that followed to be her true self. Today, Amanda and her wife, Zoe, their daughter, Alexis, and their two sons are happier than ever. The Knoxes may sound like a complicated family—but they're not. They love and support each other like any other family. They also educate others about LGBTQ+ rights and speak out about transgender issues.

Our issue is
LGBTQ+ rights.

I interviewed Amanda, Zoe, and Alexis together. I'm so honoured they shared their story with me. Alexis (who's now 14) told me that before she came out as a transgender girl, she was depressed and anxious all the time.

"I didn't even know why for the longest time. Then, when I was 11, we were shopping for Pink Shirt Day and there was nothing pink in the boys' section, and we were talking about how gender roles shouldn't play a part in things and how everyone should be free to be who they are. I guess that really tipped the bucket over and I sent an email to [Amanda and Zoe] and that was my coming out. I said, 'All I want is to be a girl more than anything else in the world' and here I am."

It must have taken a lot of courage to write that email. Alexis told me she had read horror stories online of families rejecting their transgender children and throwing them out of the house.

"I thought I might be way worse off trying to be myself than being this boy everyone assumed I was. I was really nervous to come out, but when I did it was great because I felt loved and welcomed and everything was wonderful."

As a family, they decided to share Alexis's story on Amanda's blog. When I asked Amanda why,

A transgender person is a person whose gender identity (how they feel in their brain and heart) is different from the way their body is: for example, when a person with a boy's anatomy feels like a girl inside.

she told me she wanted to write about their experience because there weren't many stories online of parents accepting their transgender children.

"I thought, 'We need more stories of families leading with love and not with fear or bigotry or misunderstanding.' Our life isn't perfect. It's messy, and it's very imperfect. I couldn't imagine this any other way, though, because when I started researching transgender issues, I looked at the statistics and they were terrifying—sky-high suicide rates and bullying rates and assaults and murders—and I thought, 'This is not the world I want my child to grow up in.'"

Amanda felt like she had two options: sit back, hide, and hope the world got better or try to make the world better by sharing their story. It wasn't really a choice for her. Amanda said there's a lot of negativity online, but the positive people far outnumber the negative. Love is louder than hate.

"There are so many people who want to learn. We have met both online and offline now people and families who have made the decision to come out after reading my blog."

❝ We need more stories of families leading with love and not with fear or bigotry or misunderstanding. ❞

Amanda Knox

Our gift is Storytelling through blogging, public speaking, and advocacy.

Zoe explained that seeing Alexis become happier and grow into the young woman she's become made it impossible for her to keep living a lie. She has known she was a girl since she was about seven years old.

"I just sure didn't look like one. I got bullied a lot, so I quickly knew not to express that and to hide it. I hid that my whole life because it wasn't socially acceptable. I stuffed it in the closet and left it there for 20 years, which was really difficult. I shut down my emotions to get through the pain, but then, of course, you can't feel the joy or the happiness."

In 2015, Zoe came out to Amanda and their family as a transgender woman. Amanda wrote that she felt many things: betrayed, hurt, devastated, angry, and scared. She wasn't sure if they would get through it, but they did, and they are stronger and happier than ever.

"In some ways, we are a normal, typical family. We're still two parents and three kids. We have a house in the suburbs, the kids go to school, we watch a lot of shows, and the house is really messy. We stand out in some ways, but we blend in in others."

I asked Amanda what we can do if we hear friends, family, or classmates say negative things about transgender people. Amanda said to speak up.

"You and I are both strong allies and we're informed. If you're at a party, school, etc., and the transphobic comments come out—because as far as they know, there are no transgender people around and they're going to speak their minds—that's where we get to infiltrate and correct. That's where we say, 'Do you know any transgender people? Have you ever talked to any transgender people?' It's really great to have opinions on things, but it's really important to have informed opinions."

Alexis said that it's important to start conversations in your community, your group of friends, and your family.

"Tell people these issues matter and you should care about them and we need to change things. Just a 'Hey, this matters in the workplace' could mean that another transgender person comes out, another gay person is accepted, another person can live their life happy."

The change is creating a society that is accepting of all people.

Amanda Knox

HANNAH'S REFLECTION

HOW TO BE AN ALLY

Since I started my blog, I have always made it a point to find and read other blogs. Amanda's blog, Maven of Mayhem, is one of my favourites. She is a master storyteller who writes with humour and honesty. Through her blog, she opens minds and hearts everywhere.

Amanda proves just how important storytelling is. It's through our stories we can create community, and it's through community we can create change. The support Amanda, Alexis, and Zoe receive from their community—both on- and offline—has created that ripple effect.

I'll start with Alexis, because the support she has received beyond the walls of her family home has been an important part of how she sees herself and her ability to be an advocate not just for herself but for others like her and for their families, schools, and local communities. There's a saying, "love is louder than hate," and that is especially true when love and acceptance come in large numbers and from influential voices.

In June 2016, Amanda, Alexis, Ashley Rose Murphy, and I were all part of a special project with Microsoft called #My24Hrs. Microsoft selected six change-makers from across Canada to share how we were using our time wisely to give back and create change. The idea was to spark both conversations and ideas around how we can best use our time. Microsoft created videos and a social media campaign through which our stories were shared. Our messages were amplified because of the support from Microsoft.

A few months later, Amanda and Alexis were given the biggest dose of community support they could imagine when Microsoft and WE Day invited them to share their story on the WE Day stage as part of Microsoft's partnership with WE. It was the first time that LGBTQ+ stories were highlighted in this way. To this day, Amanda's tweet about that day remains pinned to the top of her Twitter feed, which speaks to how much it meant to her.

Support from family and community can be everything to someone who is seeking to be accepted for who they are.

Which brings me to Zoe. Once Zoe was secure in the support she received from her family, she was ready to take the next steps and start living fully as Zoe. That needed to include where she spent most of her time—work. Amanda wrote on her blog:

Amanda Jette Knox ✔
@MavenOfMayhem

Today I asked 18,000 people if acceptance & understanding for #trans people was finally happening. They cheered. Loudly. #WEDayVancouver 🖤

2016-11-03, 10:53 PM

Tweet your reply

> [Zoe] works at a large technology company, managing a team of software developers in a predominantly male office environment. She's known many of her co-workers and employees for 15 or so years. They have called her "he" and "him" and "Mr." for a very long time. How would they handle the change?

Zoe started, like Alexis did, by reaching out with an email (to her colleagues), and in return, she received messages filled with support and encouragement. She took a week off and worked from home as she prepared herself for that first day back at the office. Despite all of those kind emails, Zoe was nervous to make her entrance. Sometimes showing up is hard.

In my favourite blog post that Amanda has published on her blog—one that was picked up and went viral thanks to Upworthy, Buzzfeed, and countless others—she described how Zoe was welcomed to the office in the warmest way. Her workspace was decorated for a party, and her name, Zoe, was posted everywhere. There were flowers and cards, too. There was literally icing on the cake when she walked into a "meeting" that was actually a surprise party. In typical Amanda style, the post ended with this message:

It's a lot of energy to judge people, you know. It's way more fun to celebrate and support them for who they are. Besides, we have cupcakes.

The support that Alexis and Zoe received at home gave them both the opportunity and courage to live their lives as their true and authentic selves. The support and acceptance they have received from their immediate and larger communities has encouraged them to become storytellers who lead with love as advocates and allies.

Amanda, Zoe, and Alexis are not only examples but leaders when it comes to what it looks like to be allies. Amanda takes her microphone—sometimes literally as a public speaker, but also on her blog and social media—to tell stories that give way to understanding, acceptance, and inclusivity.

Amanda Knox

"BE GRATEFUL.
BE THANKFUL."

Michael
"Pinball"
Clemons

MICHAEL "PINBALL" CLEMONS:
PHILANTHROPIST, MOTIVATIONAL SPEAKER, GIVER

Michael "Pinball" Clemons is one of my favourite people. We met backstage at WE Day in 2013, and since then we've worked together on local initiatives to support youth, education, and community. When I think about motivational speakers, he is the first person who comes to mind, and when I think about selfless people, he is top of that list, too. There's something about Pinball—when you're around him, you're the best version of yourself, and then when you leave him, you want to be even better.

He earned the nickname "Pinball" soon after being drafted to play football for the Toronto Argonauts. After the first few practices, his coach said, "We have this new guy that bounces around like a pinball." He's been "Pinball" ever since. He's also a two-time CFL All-Star, three-time Grey Cup champion as a player, and a one-time Grey Cup champion as head coach with the Argos. He is one of Canada's most celebrated and respected athletes.

Off the field, though, he's also one of our greatest role models. Pinball's life story is one of hard work, perseverance, determination, and optimism.

My issue is injustice done to children & women.

Whenever Pinball speaks, he begins by sharing a bit about his life growing up in Florida. The hero of the story is always the same—his mom.

"I was born to a single parent in the projects, but I do believe that's often overstated. I never thought of myself as poor. My mom provided everything I could possibly need."

He admits that his dad is often dismissed in the story. "When you're standing up and speaking to a group, you're just trying to get a point across and say it as quickly as possible, but my dad actually was the first family member—first one in his family—to graduate from university and was a tremendous role model and leader in his community."

Realizing that both his parents had success in life was motivating and important. But as Pinball told me, his mom was always his champion.

"She was amazing. The sacrifices she made were unbelievable to help me to grow and become a young person who had choices and opportunities—better said, a wealth of choices and opportunities—because she stressed education, because she was so diligent in supporting me in my sporting activities. She missed one game from the time I was eight years old until I was 18 years old."

Pinball wants to help young people reach their potential. Together with his wife, Diane (who, after 25 years of marriage and three children, he still calls his "bride"), he co-founded the Pinball Clemons Foundation. The foundation's goal is to empower youth through education, support, and mentorship. I told Pinball that what he does is amazing. He was humble.

"I have never achieved very much by myself, but together our foundation has now funded over 200 schools in developing countries, and does what we believe is some very important local work, specifically with the Ambassador School in Toronto. It's a school partnered with the Children's Aid Foundation. The kids who go there have been in foster care. Many times they've escaped or are in abusive situations and have had to overcome quite a bit in their lives."

It's difficult to concentrate on schoolwork when you're experiencing trauma and adversity. Many students at the Ambassador School are getting high school credits for the first time and are planning to pursue post-secondary education.

The Pinball Clemons Foundation ...

- has built 231 schoolhouses/classrooms in developing countries around the world
- is currently adopting an entire village in Kenya with a five-year commitment
- has provided 100 scholarships for students who are thriving academically but struggling financially in Toronto
- for the past three years, has provided funding to keep an alternative school open for youth in care who are too traumatized to go to mainstream school
- has donated over 771,000 kg (1.7 million lb) of food over three years to 14 food banks across the greater Toronto area
- every summer for the past eight years, has sent 400 kids from the Jane–Finch community to summer camp for six weeks

Michael "Pinball" Clemons

My gifts are Support, resources, & mentorship.

I've heard some of the students tell their stories at Pinball's Imagine Gala. These students are the ultimate in comeback stories. Pinball understands that with the right support and mentors, the students have opportunities they could never have imagined.

In addition to the power of education, Pinball believes in the power of kindness and community.

"Kindness actually makes us rich. It makes our community full. It energizes us. It replenishes us. It builds us up. If all we do is take from our community, then our community becomes depleted, because life is about people, not stuff. If no one ever did anything for themselves and all they did was focus on everybody else, we would never have anything to worry about because we would always be taken care of."

Pinball believes that being kind is the ultimate thing you can do, and that we all have something to give. He is so passionate about this that he created an initiative called JUST GIVE. (More on that in the following pages.)

"When people are reaching out, when they're engaging, they are much less likely to feel separated, to feel alone, to have these different feelings of anxiety and anxiousness. It is that interconnectedness that makes us have value and feel value."

66 If no one ever did **anything for themselves** and all they did was **focus on everybody else**, we would never have anything to worry about because **we would always be taken care of. 99**

Pinball is one of the most generous, kind, and positive people I've ever met. I asked him how he manages to be like that, because some days, it's a challenge.

"An old football coach said, 'Any day above ground shows potential.' For me, it really is a lifestyle. It's a choice. And even when you don't feel like it, if I make that choice, a bad day will be better. A good day will be greater. It's a matter of discipline and self-control. Being positive, I believe, is simply making the best of any situation."

I've learned a lot from Pinball over the years, but what I take away every time I'm with him is realizing how much our attitude affects the people around us. Sometimes when we're at an event, I like to take a step back and watch him. He takes the time to talk to everyone, and when people talk to him, he really listens and gives them his full attention, as if each one is the only person in the room.

The change is providing youth access to education.

JUST GIVE & KINDRAISING

One of the myths I encounter a lot is that changing the world takes big actions—that little actions can't change the world. It's this kind of thinking that often stops people from taking action. It might also be fair to say this kind of thinking sometimes stops people from recognizing that they are, in fact, already creating change with their everyday actions.

Pinball is someone who understands that everything makes a difference. Through his JUST GIVE initiative, he inspires people to smile and be kind to one another with the simplest acts, whether that's holding the door open for someone or giving them a compliment or a high-five. Pinball believes we all have something to give, and that giving begets giving.

JUST GIVE is a campaign designed to inspire kindness throughout our communities, and when I went out to join Pinball and his team, I just knew I was part of something that was making a difference. We gathered in the morning at Union Station in Toronto—Canada's busiest commuter hub at the busiest time. Our goal was simple: hold doors open, smile, say good morning, and give high-fives. We were like a flash mob of kindness. The idea was to send people off to work or to school with smiles on their faces, having been on the receiving end of a random act of kindness. The hope was that they would pass it on and we would create a ripple effect of kindness that would spread through the city.

When people are kind to others and do something awesome for them, they pay it forward and it creates a cycle of good vibes that is potentially endless.  Now, *that* changes the world because it can make the world a brighter and better place through people doing bright, awesome things out of the kindness of their hearts. So, a particular action might not change the world, but it does change people and people change communities.

JUST GIVE was a whole week of actions like that, and each one inspired me. By the end of the week, I felt like I was on a new mission. JUST GIVE brought together so many of the ideas I believe in: that small actions create big change; that kind actions + thoughtful people = compassionate communities; and that these things aren't always about donating or raising money.

Help us spread
a little
KINDNESS
today!
#JUSTGIVE

"GIVING IN ITS PUREST SENSE IS BEST REFLECTED bY THOSE SPONTANEOUS MOMENTS OF kindNESS."

-Michael "Pinball" CLEMONS #JUSTGIVE

One of my favourite things about Pinball is how enthusiastic he is. His smile brightens up the room every time he walks in, and he is always kind to people. His positivity motivates me to have a more positive outlook on life and do my best to be friendly to everyone I meet, no matter what. I have made it my mission to do an act of kindness for at least four people every day. Not only has doing this made others feel good about their day, but I can tell that I have been smiling more doing these acts of kindness, and now I don't think I can stop. But that's not a bad thing.

After sitting with all of this for a while and having endless conversations over dinners with my family, I figured it out: **kindraising**. That's what we were doing, and that's what we needed to do more of. More of that would mean more and bigger ripples that would reach more people.

I come from a family that lives digitally—we all blog and use social media for work and play—and once we came up with the word and idea of kindraising, a ripple effect all its own was unleashed. We registered the domain name for a website, secured the Twitter handle, and set out to define what we were going to do. Naturally, it started with a blog post....

Posted on September 8, 2015

I believe we all have something to give, and that creating change isn't always about fundraising, and that giving a little kindness goes a long way. We need to raise more kindness, compassion, and empathy to replace hate, indifference, and apathy. That is KINDRAISING.

Kindraising is all about acts of kindness—random, planned, or organized. Kindraising is not about me—it's about everyone—because that is what it's going to take to create the culture shift that we need. I created the site to share the stories, experiences, and ideas of people that have given, received, or witnessed kindness—the actions that have changed someone's mood, day, or circumstance.

I have travelled across North America and met people of all ages who are dedicated to taking action to make a difference in their community:

Students collecting food for their local food banks, young girls donating their hair to make wigs for children going through chemotherapy, groups of women who get together to knit scarves for the homeless, families who spend time cooking and serving food at soup kitchens, and I know of a 70-year-old man who has volunteered more than 1,000 hours at a nursing home. These are just some of the people and actions that inspire me. You are never too young or too old to give and we should all give what we can, when we can and how we can.

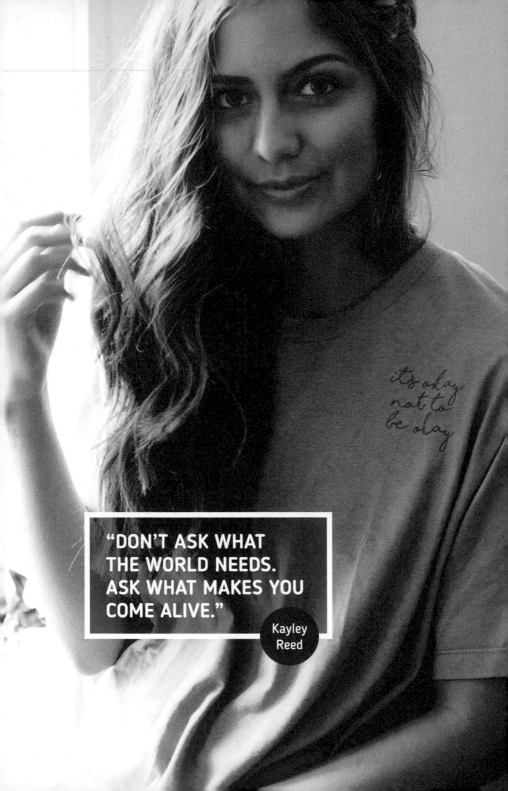

"DON'T ASK WHAT
THE WORLD NEEDS.
ASK WHAT MAKES YOU
COME ALIVE."

Kayley
Reed

KAYLEY REED:

CO-FOUNDER, CEO, & CREATIVE DIRECTOR OF WEAR YOUR LABEL

It's okay not to be okay. *This was not an overnight discovery or an easy learning for Kayley Reed, but I am so glad that this realization has become Wear Your Label.*

Kayley and her friend Kyle MacNevin launched Wear Your Label in 2014 with the aim to create awareness and start conversations around mental health. It began as a line of T-shirts with simple yet strong statements, such as "It's okay not to be okay," "Your body is not the enemy," "Sad but rad," and "Self-care isn't selfish." Today, Wear Your Label is more than a T-shirt company, and its collection of stigma-fighting products includes phone cases, baseball hats, and bracelets. Wear Your Label is also more than products; it's a movement.

I am inspired by Kayley's honesty, courage, and passion. She launched WYL from an idea that would free herself and others from hiding. Kayley is one of the most visible advocates for mental health and a true example that it really is okay not to be okay.

My issue is mental health.

Kayley told me that she experienced depression in high school and university, but didn't feel comfortable sharing that with anyone.

"I didn't have anybody in my life who was talking about mental health, and I didn't learn about mental illness in school. At the same time, I was this straight-A student. I was super involved in everything, and on the outside looking in, everything in my life was perfect. But I was miserable."

During her first year of university, Kayley would cry herself to sleep. She didn't know why. Kayley visited a doctor who told her she had depression and gave her some medicine, but that was it. She kept her depression a secret for three years, and it eventually developed into an eating disorder. Her life began to change when she started going to group therapy.

"I met other girls who had eating disorders and body image issues. It was the first time in my life I realized how common it was for people to go through that or that it was related to mental illness."

Kayley and Kyle volunteered at a mental health organization.

"We were both struggling with our own mental health challenges and both loved fashion. We thought, 'What if we could create a clothing line to make mental illness more visible? So people could see it.'"

One in five people live with mental illness, but five in five have mental health.

They found their spark. "We didn't know what it looked like at the time. We just had this idea and wanted to make it real."

They were putting the idea of Issue + Gift = Change into action. Change happens when you discover your issue and match it with your gift: that talent, skill, or passion you have.

They taught themselves how to sew and screen print. They weren't receiving many orders, so they weren't making much money. Then that all changed.

"One day we got an email from a woman at the *Today Show*. She wanted to show our story on today.com and we were like, 'This is amazing!'"

They said yes, and from that moment on, it wasn't just a couple of university students making and selling T-shirts. Kayley had to start looking at this T-shirt company as a growing business, and she was not simply the designer anymore—she was CEO. The *Today Show* was "the catalyst for the other growth that we've had. We got invited to show at NY Fashion Week."

As you might expect, the models for any WYL runway, event, or website embody the label's message, and I love that. WYL models are actual role models in every way—inside and out. The only requirement is that they wear their label.

My gifts are Storytelling & creating.

"Being able to build something I'm so passionate about, and see it grow, is what actually helped me the most in my recovery. More than any doctor, more than anything else, just building WYL. I am the happiest I've ever been. I'm the healthiest I've ever been, and am just building on what's next for WYL."

WYL has impacted so many people's lives. Kayley told me she gets emails every day from people saying they finally feel comfortable talking about their mental health challenges thanks to WYL.

"I want that to happen to more people. I want to keep sharing those messages and start sharing other people's stories, too, because it's not just about my story. It's about creating the tools to help other people tell their stories."

Kayley has inspired others to find their issue relating to mental health, take action on it with their gift, and help erase the stigma. I asked Kayley what she thought about the stigma associated with mental illness.

"There's definitely a general idea of what mental illness looks like, specifically in the media. It's portrayed in a certain way, either as the crazy person or as the person from a really bad background. But anybody can have it. It's not someone's choice. Mental illness doesn't discriminate.

 Mental illness **doesn't** discriminate.

It's frustrating when people stereotype mental health and assume things about people they don't know well enough.

Kayley said one of the main reasons she and Kyle started WYL is to make mental health visible in a positive way.

"When you break your arm, you get a cast, and the cast is like a symbol to the world that you're healing. It's not like that for mental illness. There's nothing you can physically see to know a person might be struggling, but they're getting better. What our clothing kind of does is bring back the visibility to an invisible issue."

Kayley told me the online community is a huge support system for her. She said she wouldn't be where she is without it.

"You can't do it alone. It's so cliché, but we're just so much more powerful when we do things in collaboration."

I have felt this way since my journey started. You can't do everything alone. You cannot be successful by yourself. It helps to know people are ready to listen and help. My online community makes me realize I'm not alone, and there are people I can talk to who have interests and passions similar to mine.

The change is helping to remove the stigma associated with mental illness.

Kayley Reed

CALLING ALL FRIENDS!

Kayley is an example of someone who under-stands the value of community. One of the most special communities for me has been at ME to WE's leadership facility, Take Action Camp. Don't get fooled by the name. It may sound really offi-cial and, well, boring, but it is the furthest thing from it. I spent a week there five summers in a row. At Take Action Camp, I've met people who have either found their issue and are already taking action or have come because they want to find their spark. One day, I learned something that I want to share with you.

Our facilitator had gathered us together for an activity one afternoon. They took us out to the field and blindfolded us. My group couldn't help but stifle a laugh at the situation, either because we were a bit nervous or because we probably looked ridiculous. Maybe both. Our facilitator led each of us into a roped-off square space and we were told to put our hands on the rope. The task they gave us seemed simple enough: find your way out.

I felt confident I could do it. I love a good challenge. The rules puzzled me a bit, though:

- You couldn't let go of the rope until you got out.
- You couldn't go under or over the rope.
- You couldn't push your way out.

We started the challenge. As time went on and I heard more and more people getting out, I was beginning to get confused and, I'll admit, a little frustrated. "What am I doing wrong?" I thought.

"If we can't let go of the rope, how are we supposed to get out?" I felt like I had walked the entire perimeter of the square holding that rope and I was pretty sure there wasn't an opening. I was at a point where I had had enough. I took a deep breath and asked my facilitator for help. He immediately came over to me and showed me the way out. "That's it? What was the point of the challenge if you had to ask for help to get out?"

After the last person of my group was out, our facilitator explained what the activity was all about—you can't do everything alone. Sometimes, you can only reach your goal with help.

None of us can create change in our home and community (let alone the world) without help. Some of the issues (or challenges) we need to solve are so big and overwhelming that we can only work toward the solutions with help.

Aha.

Ask any change-maker or activist, or anyone who's achieved something, what the number one thing that helped them through their journey is, and I'm sure that nine out of 10 will say "support." Having spoken to many, and speaking also from my own experience, I can verify this.

Everyone has different gifts and skills they can bring to the table. For example, when you're launching an initiative or a campaign at school or in your community, look for those people who have gifts—skills or talents—that can help you. Here's a short list of some of the gifts (or help) you might need:

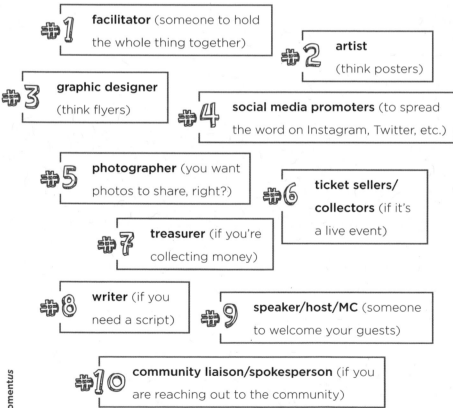

#1 **facilitator** (someone to hold the whole thing together)

#2 **artist** (think posters)

#3 **graphic designer** (think flyers)

#4 **social media promoters** (to spread the word on Instagram, Twitter, etc.)

#5 **photographer** (you want photos to share, right?)

#6 **ticket sellers/collectors** (if it's a live event)

#7 **treasurer** (if you're collecting money)

#8 **writer** (if you need a script)

#9 **speaker/host/MC** (someone to welcome your guests)

#10 **community liaison/spokesperson** (if you are reaching out to the community)

Wait a second, did I say "short" list? See? You can't do all of this by yourself. You need to ask for help.

Don't think you can do everything yourself because let me tell you something, you can't. And let me remind you, "can't" is not a word or an idea I use often, so believe me when I say it. You can't. You can't start (or finish) anything for that matter, whether it's a fundraising campaign or a talent show, alone. But please, please, don't let it stop you from starting. Ask for help.

All of the people I have included in this book have done such incredible things, but they had help from people who possessed different skills that helped them in different ways. Spencer and his friends could not have climbed Mount Kilimanjaro without each other. Corinne and Katrine launched Warm Winters together and received further support from a mentor. Malala relies on her father for support—in fact, you rarely see one without the other. Through Project Jenga, Mitch raised a million dollars to fund the building of a school—with, that's right, a whole lot of help.

I'm going to let you in on something: public speaking is hard work, and I get help in many ways. When I spoke at WE Day for the first time, I had help from a whole team of people. It was a process—a lot of time, energy, and work. With my first WE Day speech, multiple people from the WE Day team worked with me, not just writing and editing the script, but preparing my presentation of that script. I worked with the WE Day producers and also with Marc Kielburger; they all helped me be the best I could be. At the time, I had given only one speech, and it was at a school assembly in front of 300 students. WE Day was a stadium filled with 20,000 students at one time. Also, that first WE Day speech involved a lot more than speaking. There was a youth string

Kayley Reed

orchestra that played "Don't You Worry Child" behind us as we spoke, so our timing had to be in sync. While public speaking and the rest of what I do comes naturally to me, it is work, and it's a skill I have developed and worked hard at, not only with practice, but with help.

From that first time and beyond, I have been lucky and proud to call Marc Kielburger my mentor. I am on the ME to WE Speakers Bureau, and I travel across North America to give keynote speeches to schools, groups, and organizations. The talk I give is 45 minutes long and includes a multimedia presentation. Marc has been there with me every step of the way, helping me to develop the content and delivery of my speeches. You know that saying "It takes a village"? For real, it does.

I spend most Saturdays with Micah, my speech coach, to help strengthen the impact of how I say what I say to inspire people. I would not be able to do what I do today without the support of these people.

There are other ways and places to find the help you need to take action on issues you're passionate about. There are many organizations that have information, resources, and tools ready and waiting for someone like you to take action. When I was just getting started and looking for ways to make a difference, that's what I did. I still do. Whatever your issue is, an organization in your community or online is working on the same thing. Many of them, like WE, Warm Winters, and Pink Shirt Day, have campaign toolkits that are fully developed and ready to download and use at your school or in your community. They have everything you need to get started—a description of the steps to take and downloadable forms, sample letters, and posters, as well as images to share on social media. You know what these organizations are looking for? Helpers. Maybe that's you.

I promise there is nobody with all of the gifts needed to launch a successful action plan. But, hey, if you're thinking, "Nope, I'm pretty sure I have all the skills I can use all at the same time," I would love to meet you! I might need your help.

"I AM ENOUGH AS I AM."

Lily Collins

LILY COLLINS:
ACTOR, AUTHOR, ANTI-BULLYING ACTIVIST

I met Lily Collins at WE Day Seattle in 2015 when we co-hosted the Social Empowerment segment. I admit—I was pretty nervous, and I might have spent extra time rehearsing. I was a fan of Lily's movies (especially Mirror Mirror *and* Love, Rosie*). Also, my dad is a huge fan of her dad, musician Phil Collins. My dad was like "My daughter is going to be speaking with his daughter!" But when she and her mom, Jill, walked into the room to rehearse, I realized how down-to-earth and kind Lily is.*

On the WE Day stage, Lily and I talked about bullying, gender equality, and how we were both ambassadors for the anti-bullying organization Bystander Revolution. It was an inspiring conversation, not just for the audience but for me as well. Today, I love that I can call Lily my friend. We connect through social media and DM each other when something really cool in our lives happens.

What I admire about Lily is how hardworking she is and the way that she uses social media to spread positive vibes, and by doing so encourages others to do the same.

My issues are Spreading positivity & inspiring confidence.

Born in England, Lily moved to the United States when she was five years old and felt like she didn't fit in from the start.

"I had a different accent. I looked a little different than a typical Los Angeles American look. And when I moved here, I just wanted to find friends and fit in. I looked different than a lot of the kids here, because I had these thicker eyebrows. People were making fun of me; they were commenting on them. I couldn't get away from them. I couldn't hide from them."

Lily told me she tried to change how she looked because she wanted to blend in. But as she got older, she began to realize that when *she* met new people she looked for the thing that distinguished *them* from others.

"My mum had always taught me this quote: 'The quirky things that make you different are what make you beautiful.' You don't really register what that means until you start to acknowledge that you yourself are appreciating the differences in other people. And then you go, 'Well, if I can appreciate their differences, what about mine?' You start to realize that those things that were insecurities for you end up being these amazing, beautiful, different things about you that make you stand out."

In her book, *Unfiltered: No Shame, No Regrets, Just Me*, Lily starts conversations about bullying, eating disorders, kindness, and how we can all make our little part of the world a better place. She also wrote about her insecurities and struggles. Lily devoted an entire chapter to her eating disorder. I think it's brave of Lily to be so open in her book and online. I asked her what made her do it.

"I think I was reaching a point where I realized as a person, maybe I'm someone that needs to just be held accountable in order to really make a change within myself. And it's so easy to keep things inside and keep things secret, and when you do that, you're the only person that can hold yourself accountable. But there comes a point when, as you get older, maybe a little extra help is not so bad, you know; accepting help is not a weakness."

Lily stars in a movie, titled *To the Bone*. In it, she portrays a 20-year-old young woman struggling with severe anorexia. This role is a full-circle moment for Lily, who told me it gave her both courage and closure.

My gift is using my voice to encourage others to use theirs.

Lily Collins

Lily said that the more she talked with people the more she related to others, and vice versa.

"I was reminded that I wasn't alone in that struggle. The point of me writing the book was to make others feel like they weren't alone, and yet I'm still being given this gift every time I talk to someone who's read it, that I'm still not alone, too. It's this amazing feeling of being united with people you never would have thought you'd have anything in common with."

Lily is a big communicator on social media and loves the idea of connecting with her friends and fans online.

"I think it's a great tool to use. I feel very fortunate to be sur-rounded by such positivity on my social media. Of course, there are going to be bad things here and there, like negative comments, but for the most part, I feel very lucky and grateful that most of it is very inspiring and positive. And so I respond to positivity. If I see anything negative, I don't interact with that because I don't want to spend the energy giving back to negativity."

I love scrolling through Lily's feeds. Her messages are full of positivity and inspiration. And I agree with her: why spend time dealing with the negative stuff when you could be talking about the positive stuff?

❝ If I see anything negative,
I don't interact with that because
I don't want to spend the energy giving back to negativity. ❞

The change is inspiring others to use their voices.

Lily said that people on Instagram inspired her to share her story.

"My book is so heavily inspired [by people] on Instagram and how they were so active about sharing their stories. And they're not anonymous; they've got their photos next to their stories, and I think it's so powerful. And I thought, 'Well, if they're being so brave, why can't I be so brave?' I thought it was really, really important to participate in that honesty."

Lily is now trying to live her life as *unfiltered* as possible.

"I'm literally putting out there what it is that I am. And that's my past, my present, and what I want for my future. I'm not ashamed of what I went through anymore. I'm not afraid to talk about the things that made me who I am, and even if that paints me in a picture that's not perfect, it's going to be raw and emotional."

Being unfiltered is about being open to talking about whatever it is you want to talk about and not filtering your words or silencing your voice. As Lily told me:

"It's okay to say things that not everyone's going to agree with, but as long as it's coming from a solid, positive place of love within yourself, then no one can fault you for that."

Lily Collins

REFLECTION ON REJECTION

One of the things I most admire about Lily is how open she is. If you've read her book, *Unfiltered*, you've gotten to know this about her, too. For Lily, living unfiltered means not being ashamed of your experiences and, more than that, owning them. In the end, it's about recognizing that you learn something from everything you go through. As Lily says, "There is no shame in anything that you go through, because it's what creates who you are today."

Lily and I had an interesting conversation about what happens when things don't go your way—when things don't turn out as you planned or hoped.

It's easy to look at Lily's career and see all the amazing roles she has been able to play: Snow White in *Mirror Mirror*, Clary Fray in *The Mortal Instruments: City of Bones*, Marla Mabrey in *Rules Don't Apply*, and Ellen in *To the Bone*. But when you look her up on IMDB, what you don't see are all the roles she auditioned for and didn't get. Lily told me that in acting you hear "no" a lot more than "yes" and that's just the way it is. It's not personal. It's not that they don't like YOU; it's just that the role doesn't fit you (and vice versa). So you keep looking and keep auditioning for the roles you feel good about, and you keep working on yourself—your skills and talents.

I couldn't help but think how this related to my own experience as an activist and also the experiences of my peers. It's not easy, whether you're fundraising for a campaign or asking for support in other ways, like starting a club in your school or community. You hear "no" a lot. And like for Lily, it's not personal. Often there are not enough resources to go around.

One of the best pieces of advice I have ever been given was from Randy Lennox, who at the time was the president of Universal Music Canada—so this is a guy who has been on both the giving and the receiving side of "no." Randy told me:

"No" is a request for more information.

What this means to me is that the person saying "no" might be saying "no" because they don't have enough information, or the right information, to say "yes." What you need to do next is figure out why they said "no." Is it because they don't have enough understanding of the issue? Is it because they don't have enough resources to give you? Is it because there is not enough time? Is it because they don't feel connected to your issue or project? It could be any of these reasons.

So at that point, you can either give up and move on or you can, as Randy suggested, give the person more information. Not just any information; it must be the right information. This is where you really need to know your stuff and your audience. What do they care about and how can you draw a connection between what they care about and what you care about?

Lily shared with me that she looks at every rejection as a learning experience that she brings into her next audition. Sometimes rejection is hard to take, and Lily is not saying that rejection doesn't affect her and she doesn't feel it. She does, I do, and you do, too. Totally okay. But then you move on and figure out what you learned, what you might do differently next time, or what knowledge or skill you want to work on. Then start plotting your next move.

"BE THE CHANGE."

Marc &
Craig
Kielburger

MARC & CRAIG KIELBURGER:

HUMANITARIANS, CO-FOUNDERS OF WE

"Born out of a dream. Two brothers fuelled by the desire for change, by the hope that the world can be a better place. They called it WE Day." To me, these are powerful words in the promo video for WE Day, and by now, you know that these two brothers are Marc and Craig Kielburger, co-founders of WE.

They live their mantra, "Be the change," and in doing so, they have set my generation up to create our own change. From humble beginnings around their kitchen table, they have inspired and empowered not only youth, but also businesses, families, and entire communities.

During my first WE Day Tour, I spoke at the Celebration Dinner, the night before every WE Day. I was 10 years old, and Marc helped me write that speech. The room was filled with adults—partners and donors. There was a line at the very end of my speech: "When you believe in a young person, you become a hero." There is no one who believes in young people with as much passion as Marc and Craig Kielburger. They are my heroes.

Throughout my years with WE, I've gotten to know Marc and Craig and their family, and I'm thrilled to end my book with their interview. Craig started off with a bit of Kielburger family history.

"My parents come from humble beginnings. My maternal grandfather died unexpectedly at a young age, leaving my grandmother to fend for herself and her children. My mother, Theresa, was nine years old and was forced to take on a job to help support the family. Their situation was dire. One summer, they slept in a tent; another year, they dined on baloney sandwiches for Christmas. Oftentimes they went without. Life was a daily struggle."

Their mother's experience shaped how she and her husband raised their children. Craig told me he and his brother were fortunate—they were never homeless, hungry, or wanting for anything. However, their mother exposed them to that reality during visits to downtown Toronto. She would start conversations with people who were homeless.

"Our mom would use this opportunity to teach us. She would walk on over, strike up a conversation, asking them their name, if they had anything to eat that day, if they had a place to go for the night. She put a name to the person on the street. She humanized them and included us in their short conversations."

Craig and Marc's mom did that because she didn't want her sons to "walk on by" someone in need. It was a powerful lesson about having empathy for others, and it remained with the brothers their whole lives.

In fact, it was empathy that 12-year-old Craig felt when he read the story of Iqbal Masih in the newspaper. It was the reality of this 12-year-old boy on the other side of the world, who had spent years as a child labourer, escaped, spoke out, and was then killed. It was empathy that sparked Craig's action. He could not walk on by.

Marc explained to me that WE is more than the name of their organization. It's bigger than that—it's a philosophy and a way of living.

"It is the idea that by focusing on 'we'—the people in our communities—rather than on 'me,' we can change the world for ourselves and others. We believe that the greatest impact is made when we decide to make change part of our everyday lives and when we decide to do it together with our communities, through the choices we make, the way we treat people, and how we choose to spend our time and resources."

66 We believe that **the greatest impact is made** when **we decide to make change** part of our **everyday lives** and when we decide **to do it together with our communities. 99**

My favourite question of our interview is one that I asked them both to answer in private: "How would you describe your brother?"

About Craig, Marc said, "Hands down, Craig is the most passionate and hardworking person I know—and I'm not just saying that because he's my brother! He deeply believes in the work we do, and has since we were kids just about to embark on this journey. His fearless conviction and relentless positivity are contagious, which makes him an incredibly inspiring leader, of course, but also an amazing person."

About his older brother, Craig said, "Marc inspired me when I was growing up. His dedication to environmental causes lit the fire within me to take an interest in social causes and he taught me how to take action. Doing service work brought us closer together as kids, and now that we're adults, our service work through WE continues to keep our bond strong."

They both said that they feel lucky to have each other as support and inspiration, and Craig added that "being able to face the world's challenges side by side with my brother has been a dream come true."

They have been side by side through it all, literally, whether it's together on stage at WE Day or standing as each other's best man when they each got married.

Marc and Craig have given me many things—support and mentorship, empowerment, and opportunity. I have gratefully accepted these and used them on my journey to "be the change." But beyond the experiences and opportunities, if I had to name one tangible thing they have given me, it's the tool I not only use for myself but also share with others: that formula, Issue + Gift = Change.

I asked Marc to declare his Issue + Gift = Change:

"I strongly believe that anyone, no matter who they are or where they come from, can change the world. But sometimes, they might need a little help to find their spark and pinpoint the cause they're passionate about. This is my 'issue.' I've long had a love of public speaking, and I'm grateful that I have the opportunity to apply this 'gift' to inspire others to create change in their own communities.

"The speaking opportunity that gives me the greatest opportunity to create 'change' is WE Day. I get the greatest feeling from the impact that WE Day inspires, whether it's random acts of kindness or the next youth-led organization started by a 12-year-old in a school somewhere."

Issue + Gift = Change. It's all you need to get started. It's all you need to keep going.

Marc & Craig Kielburger

DISCOVERING YOUR ISSUE CAN HAPPEN WHEN YOU LEAST EXPECT IT

On a Saturday morning in 1995, 12-year-old Craig was looking through the newspaper for the comics section when he found his issue in a headline: "Battled child labour, boy, 12, murdered." Those words, next to the photo of Iqbal Masih, changed Craig's life forever.

Iqbal Masih was a child labourer in Pakistan who had spent 14 hours a day, seven days a week chained to a carpet-weaving loom since the age of four. He escaped at 10 years old and began to speak out and share his story—and the stories of thousands of children like him. Iqbal became a voice that was heard all over the world. When he was 12 years old, he was shot and killed while riding his bike.

Craig was shocked at what he had read, and he began researching child labour. He asked his teacher if he could share what he was learning with his class. His teacher said "yes," and Craig said to his classmates, "This is what I know. This is what I want to do. Who wants to help?" Eleven hands were raised. They called themselves "The 12 12-Year-Olds." But they had to change the name when one of them turned 13.

Today, WE is a global movement creating change locally and globally. It all began with Craig reading Iqbal's story in the newspaper. Craig took action, and look at the impact WE has had since its founding:

WE Global Impacts

1 million people have been provided safe and **clean water**.

1,000 schools + schoolrooms have been built, giving 200,000 children access to education.

$36 million in medical supplies and equipment has provided 1 million people with healthcare.

15 million meals have been produced by farmers in WE Village Agriculture Programs.

30,000 mamas and other women are empowered with financial independence.

WE Local Impacts

771,000 Kg (1.7 million lb) of food have been collected and donated to local food banks.

27 million hours of volunteer service have been performed.

12,000 schools are part of the WE family through WE Schools.

$79.8 million has been raised for more than 2,500 charities.

Statistics provided by WE.org

That's a LOT of change from the actions of one 12-year-old.

Craig discovered that when he put together his passion for his issue, the knowledge he was building, and the support of his friends, he could create change. Back in the days when WE was called Free The Children, I would tell people that its name really meant two things. It was about freeing children, like Iqbal and the millions of other children around the world whose rights and opportunities were denied to them. It was also about freeing children from the belief they are too young to understand issues and make a difference.

Seeing those WE impacts and knowing Craig's story and how it all began proves I am not too young to change the world. And neither are you.

I have further proof through my own experience. I've travelled across North America with WE Day and the WE Create Change Tour where I met thousands of youth making local and global impacts. I saw first-hand the sustainable development in partnership with communities in Kenya.

When young people are inspired, supported, and motivated, there is no end to the change we can create.

"Never doubt
that a small
group of
thoughtful,
committed
citizens can
change the
world. ® Indeed,
it is the only
thing that
ever has."

-Margaret Mead

SOME FINAL THOUGHTS

Before I call this book finished, I want to share some of the things I'm thinking about as I'm sitting down to write these last few pages. Writing this book has been part of my journey, but it has also been a journey all its own.

In the 19 interviews, I have shared the journeys of people who are my role models. From the very beginning of my own journey, finding role models has been important to me. Through them I have discovered issues, gained confidence, been inspired, and found my path. They all have different issues, and they all have become experts, allies, leaders, and joiners. They all have different gifts they use to make a difference, and work hard to apply them to everything they do. They all have faced different challenges, and all have worked to overcome them and seek solutions.

Something that I'm realizing at this moment is that when it comes to my role models, it is *who* they are and not *what* they are that draws me to them. They all share characteristics that include compassion, resilience, and determination, and they are fuelled by the desire to be part of making the world better. When I discovered Lilly Singh, I didn't aspire to be a YouTube Creator and aim for 12 million subscribers. Lilly inspires me because of her hustle, her self-confidence, and her message of inclusivity. When I learned about Blake Mycoskie and TOMS, I didn't aspire to start a business. I admired his work ethic, the way he thinks outside the box, and the fact that he didn't listen to the skeptics. We need more people who are brave, kind, creative, curious, and hopeful. We need all of this to create the world we want to live in.

You're not too young, too old, too busy, or too cool. It's not that you're not able, not wealthy, not knowledgeable, or not popular. These are not reasons to hold yourself back from making a difference. These are all *whats*, not *whos*. If you have the characteristics that your role models do, there is nothing you can't do. Be who you want to be and be the best *you* you can be.

There's no action too small. No one sets out to change the world. Starting with small actions gave me the confidence and experience to take on bigger ones. And all of those small actions? They lead to big change. It's not just my actions that add up to big change. It's yours. It's ours. We're in this together. Moment*us*.

Issue + Gift = Change. It works. This formula for making a difference in the world is one that you'll use again and again—you'll never be too young, too old, or too anything not to.

My Issue + Gift = Change:
empowerment
+
my voice
=
more people
taking action

Now that you know the formula, you can put it to use and start taking action. Find your issue, match it with your gift, and boom—change. None of us can throw all of those starfish back into the ocean on our own, but we make a difference if we do it together.

Each and every interview I did had two common questions: "What is your Issue + Gift = Change?" and "What are your words to live by?" I'm going to wrap things up by sharing my words to live by that quote an African proverb:

66 If **you** want to **go fast**, **go alone**.
If **you** want to **go far**, **go together**. **99**

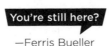

You're still here?

—Ferris Bueller

ACKNOWLEDGEMENTS

My journey has been filled with people who have believed in me, given me opportunities, and supported me along the way. There are not enough pages in any book to express my gratitude.

My family has been my biggest support system. My parents have been with me since the beginning, and I couldn't do what I do without them (and I wouldn't want to). My grandparents have always been my greatest champions, and I am eternally grateful for all their support.

To my role models, mentors, and friends who took the time and energy to share their journeys and inspiration with me, thank you.

I've had support from so many special people and organizations that have given me incredible opportunities, including the WWF, Bystander Revolution, Microsoft, RBC, and WE. Thank you to Andy Kim, Summer March, and Eason Jordan for your unending support.

Thank you to my educators, my teachers, principals, and the York Region District School Board for being so supportive.

Thank you to all the members of my WE "family," who are just amazing: from the WE Day team to the PR and Digital Teams, from Take Action Camp to the Leadership Team. A very special thank you to Yvonne Mazurak for all your time and energy with this book. *Asante Sana* to my WE "family" in Kenya: Wilson & Jackson, Tobi, Wilba, Mary, Kahato, Mama Jane and Mama Leah, Carol, the girls of Kisaruni, and the Kenyan Boys Choir.

To the team who helped me find and strengthen my voice: thank you, Lina Beaudin, Jill Pearson, Kim Plewes, Marianne Woods, and Micah Barnes.

Thank you to Lisa MacIntosh, Scott Ramsay, Vito Amati, and Mauricio Carvajal for capturing so much of my journey.

Thank you to the whole team at Nelson for making this book happen, and especially Steve Brown, Anita Reynolds MacArthur, and Tara Harte.

All my love, respect, and gratitude to Marc and Roxanne and Craig and Leysa for being a constant inspiration and for believing in me.

It's over!

—Ferris Bueller

CREDITS

This page constitutes an extension of the copyright page. We have made every effort to trace the ownership of all copyrighted material and to secure permission from copyright holders. In the event of any question arising as to the use of any material, we will be pleased to make the necessary corrections in future printings. Thanks are due to the following authors, publishers, and agents for permission to use the material indicated.

Cover Image

Used with permission of Lisa MacIntosh

Cover Text

Cover quote by Severn Cullis-Suzuki is used with permission.

Back Cover Images

(left) Photo provided by WE, (top and bottom right) Used with permission of Candace Alper

Design Elements

Tablet image: Ohmega1982/Shutterstock

Frontmatter Images

(Portrait of Hannah Alper) Used with permission of Lisa MacIntosh; (Photo of Hannah Alper in profile speaking on stage) Photo provided by WE; (Photo of Hannah being hoisted on the shoulders of Craig and Marc Kielburger) Photo provided by WE; (Portrait of Hannah and Craig Kielburger hugging) Used with permission of Vito Amati

Interior Images

4: (bottom left, top right) KateMacate/Shutterstock; (bottom middle and right, top right) Vasilyeva Larisa/Shutterstock; 5: Tom and Kwikki/Shutterstock; 7: Used with permission of Candace Alper; 8: Photo provided by WE; 9: Used with permission of Candace Alper; 12: Used with permission of Severn Cullis-Suzuki; 14: Used with permission of Severn Cullis-Suzuki; 20: Used with permission of Scott Ramsay; 23: Used with permission of Spencer West; 24: Used with permission of Candace Alper; 27: Used with permission of Spencer West; 28: Used with permission of Spencer West; 29: Used with permission of Spencer West; 30: Photo provided by WE; 32: Photo provided by WE; 36: artplay/Shutterstock; 42: Used with permission of MO Studio, LLC.;

Credits

provided by WE; 204: Photo provided by WE; 207: Photo provided by WE; 208: Photo provided by WE; 210: Photo provided by WE.

Interior Text and Graphic

4: Adapted from The Stone Thrower by Loren Eisley from The Unexpected Universe (1969, Harcourt, Brace and World; 13: Used with permission of Severn-Cullis Suzuki; 21: Used with permission of Spencer West; 31: Used with permission of Ashley Rose Murphy; 43: Used with permission of Vivienne Harr; 53: Used with permission of Blake Mycoskie; 60: Text provided by WE; 63: Used with permission of Lilly Singh; 73: Used with permission of Travis Price; 85: Used with permission of Shania Pruden; 94: Used with permission of Malala Yousafzai; 95: Used with permission of Malala Yousafzai; 103: Used with permission of Ziauddin Yousafzai; 105: Used with permission of Malala Yousafzai; 107: Used with permission of Mitch Kurylowicz; 114: Text provided by WE; 117: Used with permission of Maya Penn; 127: Used with permission of Corinne Hindes; 139: Used with permission of Brad Montague; 144: Used with permission of Brad Montague and Robby Novak; 146: Used with permission of Brad Montague; 151: Used with permission of Muzoon Almellehan; 153: Stat Box facts are from the following sources: "Syria Emergency" from UNHCR website found at http://www.unhcr.org/syria-emergency.html, "Syria Regional Refugee Response" from UNHCR website found at http://data.unhcr.org/syrianrefugees/regional.php, article entitled "Syrian refugee crisis: Facts you need to know" from World Vision website found at https://www.worldvision.org/refugees-news-stories/syria-refugee-crisis-war-facts; article entitled "A Staggering New Death Toll for Syria's War-470,000" from PBS website found at http://www.pbs.org/wgbh/frontline/article/a-staggering-new-death-toll-for-syrias-war-470000/; 156: Used with permission of the Malala Fund; 157: Used with permission of Muzoon Almellehan; 158: From "Sustainable Development Goals: 17 Goals to Transform Our World" from United Nations website found at http://www.un.org/sustainabledevelopment/education/ and "Girls Education" from Their World website found at http://theirworld.org/explainers/girls-education; 161: Text provided by WE; 163: Used with permission of Amanda Jetté Knox; 169: Used with permission of Amanda Jetté Knox; 173: Used with permission of Michael "Pinball" Clemons; 175: Used with permission of the Pinball Clemons Foundation; 180: Used with permission of the Pinball Clemons Foundation; 183: Used with permission of Kayley Reed; 195: Used with permission of Lily Collins; 200: Used with permission of Lily Collins; 203: Used with permission of Marc and Craig Kielburger; 209: Text provided by WE; 211: The Mead Trust

momentus

Go change the world!

—Hannah Alper